A Personal Journey with Martin Scorsese

Through American Movies

A Personal Journey with Martin Scorsese Through American Movies

MARTIN SCORSESE AND MICHAEL HENRY WILSON

Published in Great Britain by Faber and Faber Limited, London.
Published by Miramax Books/Hyperion in association with the British Film Institute.
Printed in Italy by Artegrafica S.p.A., Verona

Library of Congress Cataloging-in-Publication Data
Scorsese, Martin
A personal journey with Martin Scorsese through American movies /
Martin Scorsese and Michael Henry Wilson–1st. ed.
p.   cm.
Filmography p.
ISBN: 0-7868-6328-5
1. Motion pictures—United States. 2. Scorsese, Martin–Interviews. 3. Motion picture producers
and directors—United States—Interviews. I. Wilson, Michael Henry. II. Title.
PN1993.5.U6S36 1997
791.43'0973—DC21

FIRST EDITION

10 9 8 7 6 5 4 3 2 1

Page 2: Frank Sinatra and Shirley MacLaine in Vincente Minnelli's *Some Came Running*.

CONTENTS

PREFACE

As part of the celebration marking the first hundred years of cinema, I was invited by the British Film Institute in 1994 to make a documentary on American movies. From the start, my film did not intend to be a comprehensive history of American cinema, but rather, as its title indicates, a personal look at some of the American movies I have loved and which, in many cases, have had a profound impact on my own work. Even then there were too many movies to have been able to include them all.

My collaborator Michael Henry Wilson and I wrote the script for the documentary which is published in this book to go with certain film clips. At times, a clip we had chosen didn't work in juxtaposition with another or it wasn't available, and the commentary was then adapted to our choices. Thelma Schoonmaker, the film's editor, was instrumental in many of these decisions. I would like to thank Helen Morris and Michael Wilson for making our script into a book, replacing the film clips with stills. Thank you also to Bob Last, the executive producer of the documentary, to Bob and Harvey Weinstein of Miramax Films and Susan Dalsimer of Miramax Books for their help.

Martin Scorsese

In 1994, in anticipation of the centenary of the movies, the British Film Institute commissioned "The Century of Cinema," an ambitious series of documentaries in which the world's leading filmmakers were asked to interpret their native country's cinema. From day one there was no question that the American segment belonged to Martin Scorsese, the former teacher and eternal student, tireless film preservationist and his generation's most gifted moviemaker.

When Marty and I embarked upon this project, we never expected it to be so emotional. Originally, the format agreed upon was two 52–minute programs. However, as soon as we started charting our vast subject, conventional standards fell away. We had to create our own parameters, without fear of being selective or subjective. Marty could only talk about what had moved or intrigued him. This was a labor of love. It needed to breathe and grow and develop. It had to become a truly personal journey, very much like the special films we wished to celebrate. Remarkably, the BFI understood and accepted our commitment. For the next two years we roamed freely about Marty's imaginary museum, a fabulous treasure chest of thousands of pictures.

Though he would begin the journey with his childhood passion for the movies, Marty did not want to dwell on his own films, at least directly. He preferred to examine the triumphs and vicissitudes of his predecessors, the masters whose films prompted him to become a filmmaker: What price did they pay for working in Hollywood? What were their strategies? Some of the answers came from archival interviews with such key figures as John Ford and Fritz Lang, Nicholas Ray and John Cassavetes. We also called upon living witnesses, veterans like André de Toth, Gregory Peck, Arthur Penn, Billy Wilder, to evoke the old studio system, while Francis Coppola, Brian De Palma, George Lucas, came to represent the new generation which explored the electronic technologies in the seventies.

At first, we planned to include almost every director that had inspired Marty before he had embraced filmmaking. But there was no room to do justice to them all, no time to stroll and meander within the script's tight structure. All along we agonized about this, and even today Marty laments the sites we never visited, or geniuses we didn't discuss, from Ernst Lubitsch to Alfred Hitchcock to Jean Renoir . . . Fortunately, they have been duly honored elsewhere. I have to confess that our natural inclination was to favor the neglected figures—those forgotten artists or unsung craftsmen who somehow managed to communicate an original vision.

Our fervent collaboration quickly extended to Thelma Schoonmaker, Marty's film editor. She knows that a documentary has a life of its own. She compares the process to a mystery: you have to come into focus as the investigation unfolds. On such a search Thelma proved to be the ideal travel companion. Her constant probing, indefatigable experimentation, and passionate idealism helped me stay the course.

While we were editing in Las Vegas, Marty, who was also facing the epic task of shooting *Casino*, made a casual remark that startled me: "In the long run," he smiled, "this documentary is probably as important to me as a feature film—maybe more so." I think I know why. To Marty, the old masters of Hollywood are still alive; they have something to tell us, and are a constant source of inspiration. When he talks about them, he is also talking about himself. Their energy, resilience, and courage have shown him the way. How to alternate projects and make "one for them, one for yourself." Or when to be a smuggler or an iconoclast.

In delving into the past, we were in fact reaching for the present and the future. In other words, this *Personal Journey* is really designed for the new generations, particularly our young spectators, film students and aspiring filmmakers—the generations that will help the American cinema reinvent itself. My hope is that this documentary encourages them and encourages us all.

My thanks go to Francesca Gonshaw, Paul Schnee, Kristin Powers and David Cashion of Miramax Books/Hyperion; and to Paul Marshall, Peter Dyer and Conor Brady of React Design.

Michael Henry Wilson

To Zoë, (1985-1997) who watched (and sometimes slept through)
many of these movies at my side. M.S.

INTRODUCTION

MARTIN SCORSESE "Film is a disease," said Frank Capra. "When it infects your bloodstream, it takes over as the number one hormone; it bosses the enzymes; directs the pineal gland; plays Iago to your psyche. As with heroin, the antidote to film is more film."

SCENE: "DO YOU HAVE HUMILITY, MR. SHIELDS?"
Von Ellstein (Ivan Triesault), who has replaced Fred Amiel (Barry Sullivan) as the director, is setting up a shot on a sound stage. The scene is an elegant dinner. Actors sitting at a long table are in period costumes. An impatient voice calls for von Ellstein. Producer Jonathan Shields (Kirk Douglas), who has been watching from the side, looks very unhappy.
Jonathan Shields: You call that directing?
Von Ellstein: That is what I've been calling it for thirty-two years.
Shields: Why, there are values and dimensions in that scene you haven't begun to hit!
Von Ellstein: Perhaps those are not the values and dimensions I wish to hit. I could make this scene a climax. I could make every scene in this picture a climax. If I did, I would be a bad director. And I like to think of myself as one of the best. A picture all climaxes is like a necklace without a string, it falls apart.
Shields: Look, when I want a lecture on the aesthetics of motion pictures, I'll ask for it. And it won't be on my time, and it won't be a cover-up for a shallow and inept interpretation of a great scene. To be a director, you must have imagination.
Von Ellstein: Whose imagination, Mr. Shields? Yours or mine? You know what you must do, Mr. Shields, so that you'll have it exactly as you want it? You must direct this picture yourself. *(He starts moving away, but turns back to face the producer.)* To direct a picture a man needs humility. Do *you* have humility, Mr. Shields?
VINCENTE MINNELLI: *THE BAD AND THE BEAUTIFUL* (1952)

MARTIN SCORSESE When I was growing up, in the forties and fifties, I spent a lot of time in movie theaters. I became obsessed with the movies. At that time, there was nothing really available that I could find written about film—except one book— my first film book. But I couldn't afford to buy it.

13

So I borrowed it from the New York Public Library, repeatedly.

A Pictorial History of the Movies by Deems Taylor was a year-by-year history of the movies in black and white stills, up to 1949. That book cast a spell on me. I hadn't seen many of the films described in the book, so all I had at my disposal to experience them were these black and white stills. I would fantasize about them, they would play into my dreams. And I was so tempted to steal some of these pictures. A terrible urge—it was a library book after all! I confess: once or twice, I did give in to that urge.

I remember quite clearly—it was 1946 and I was four years old—when my mother took me to see King Vidor's *Duel in the Sun*. I was fanatical about Westerns. My father usually took me to see them, but this time my mother did. The movie had been condemned by the Church. "Lust in the Dust," they dubbed it. I guess she used me as an excuse to see it herself.

From the opening titles I was mesmerized. The bright blasts of deliriously vibrant color, the gunshots, the savage intensity of the music, the burning sun, the overt sexuality. A flawed film, maybe. Yet the hallucinatory quality of the imagery has never weakened for me over the years.

Jennifer Jones played a half-breed servant girl and Gregory Peck was the villain, a ruthless rancher's son who seduced her. For a child this was puzzling. How could the heroine fall for the villain? It was all quite overpowering. Frightening too. The final "duel in the sun," where Jennifer Jones shoots Gregory Peck, was too intense for this four-year-old. I covered my eyes through most of it. It seemed that the two protagonists could only consummate their passion by killing each other.

I didn't know it then, but in 1946 Hollywood had reached its zenith. Two decades later, when I embraced filmmaking, the studio system had collapsed and movie companies were taken over by giant corporations. But it was during the fifties that my passion for films grew and became a vocation. The movies then were entering a new era, the era of *The Searchers* and *The Girl Can't Help It*, *East of Eden* and *Blackboard Jungle*, *Bigger Than Life* and *Vertigo*.

My passion was fueled by all sorts of famous and infamous films—not necessarily the culturally correct ones. By films you may never have heard of: *The Naked Kiss*, *The Phenix City Story*, *The Red House* (page 16) and *Murder by Contract* (below). And by directors who are sadly forgotten: Allan Dwan, Samuel Fuller, Phil Karlson, Ida Lupino, Delmer Daves, André de Toth, Joseph H. Lewis, Irving Lerner.

SCENE: "I DON'T LIKE PIGS."

Claude (Vince Edwards), the contract killer who only believes in dollars and cents, is a mystery—even to his mentors. "I'm different," he claims. "I don't make mistakes. I eliminate personal feelings." His employer, Mr. Moon (Michael Granger) finds him too smart, too cool.

Mr. Moon (*standing by the fireplace*): Don't you get restless?

Claude (*sitting*): If I get restless, I exercise. My girl lives in Cleveland.

Mr. Moon: Well, this is not Cleveland.

Claude: I don't like pigs.

Mr. Moon: I do. Human nature.

IRVING LERNER: *MURDER BY CONTRACT* (1958)

MARTIN SCORSESE Over the years, I have discovered many obscure films and sometimes these were more inspirational than the prestigious films that received all the attention. I can't really be objective. I can only revisit what has moved or

Duel in the Sun (1946): Brilliant color and delirious music intensify the passion between Gregory Peck and Jennifer Jones.

Overlooked Films:
Samuel Fuller's *The Naked Kiss* (top),
Phil Karlson's *The Phenix City Story*
(middle) and Delmer Daves's
The Red House (bottom).

Sullivan's Travels (1941): Preston Sturges tells the story of a director (Joel McCrea, center) struggling between art and commerce.

intrigued me. This is a journey inside an imaginary museum, unfortunately one too big for us to enter each room. There is too much to see, too much to remember! So I've chosen to highlight some of the films that colored my dreams, that changed my perceptions, and in some cases even my life. Films that prompted me, for better or for worse, to become a filmmaker myself.

As early as I can remember, the key issue for me was: What does it take to be a filmmaker in Hollywood? Even today I still wonder what it takes to be a professional or even an artist in Hollywood. How do you survive the constant tug of war between personal expression and commercial imperatives? What is the price you pay to work in Hollywood? Do you end up with a split personality? Do you make one movie for them, one for yourself?

SCENE: **ART VERSUS COMMERCE**
John L. Sullivan (Joel McCrea) is a successful director who has never made a serious film. His comedies were trifles, with such titles as So Long, Sarong *and* Ants in Your Plants of 1939. *When he decides to make "a message picture, a commentary on modern conditions, a true canvas of the suffering of humanity," his producer, Mr. Hadrian (Porter Hall), and the studio head, Mr. LeBrand (Robert Warwick), think he has lost his mind. They surround Sullivan and attempt to reason him.*

Mr. Hadrian: How about making *Ants in Your Plants of 1941*? You can have Bob Hope, Mary Martin.

Mr. Le Brand: Maybe Bing Crosby.

Hadrian: The Abbey Dancers.

Le Brand: Maybe Jack Benny and Rochester.

Hadrian: A big name band and . . .

Sullivan *(coming out of his trance)***:** What? Oh no, I want to make *Oh Brother, Where Art Thou*?

PRESTON STURGES: *SULLIVAN'S TRAVELS* (1941)

1

THE DIRECTOR'S

DILEMMA

King Vidor in the editing room.

MARTIN SCORSESE I've always seen film as a means of self-expression. Most of all I've been interested in the directors, especially the ones who circumvented the system to get their vision onto the screen. At times, it seemed that everything conspired to prevent them from achieving personal expression. For there are rules, many rules, in Hollywood's power game.

A poet or a painter can be a loner, but the film director has to be, first and foremost, a team player. Particularly in Hollywood. Most important has always been the collaboration between the director and the producer. In *The Bad and the Beautiful*, the best drama about Hollywood's creative battles, Kirk Douglas (the producer) and Barry Sullivan (the director) both dream of making great films, but for their first project they have been assigned a low-budget thriller called *The Doom of the Cat Men*.

The Bad and the Beautiful (1952): Lana Turner, John Houseman, Kirk Douglas, and Vincente Minnelli (left to right) on the set.

SCENE: **"A LIFE OF ITS OWN"**

Jonathan Shields (Kirk Douglas) and Fred Amiel (Barry Sullivan) are saddled with a B-film for their first production. Sitting in a private screening room, they reflect on their predicament. Shields suddenly rises to his feet.

Jonathan Shields: Look, for five men dressed like cats on the screen, what do they look like?

Fred Amiel: Like five men dressed like cats.

Shields: When an audience pays to see a picture like this, what do they pay for?

Amiel: To get the pants scared off 'em.

Shields: And what scares the human race more than any other single thing?

He switches off the wall light. The room would be totally dark if it were not for a small desk lamp.

Amiel's voice: The dark!

Shields (*whose hand appears under the lamp*): Of course. And why? Because the dark has a life of its own. In the dark, all sorts of things come alive. (*He twitches his fingers under the lamp.*)

Amiel: Suppose we never do show the cat men? Is that what you're thinking?

Shields (*snapping his fingers*): Exactly!

Amiel: No cat men!

VINCENTE MINNELLI: *THE BAD AND THE BEAUTIFUL* (1952)

MARTIN SCORSESE Movies are a medium based on consensus. In the old days the director dealt with moguls and major studios; today he faces executives and giant corporations instead. But there is one iron rule that has never changed: every decision is shaped by the moneymen's perception of what the audience wants.

SCENE: **FACING THE PHILISTINE**

In his posh office, studio head Harry Pebbel (Walter Pidgeon) slams down an ambitious script pitched by producer Jonathan Shields (Kirk Douglas) and director Fred Amiel (Barry Sullivan).

Harry Pebbel: I've told you a hundred times, I don't want to win awards. Give me pictures that end with

The Bad and the Beautiful (1952): Lana Turner and Gilbert Roland are watched by their producer Kirk Douglas in Minnelli's insightful movie-behind-the-movie.

a kiss and black ink in the books!

Producer: I'll make this picture, Harry, or I'll quit. *(Shields and Amiel glance at each other, exasperated, almost desperate.)* This is my baby. I found it and I licked it. I want to produce it so much I can taste it!

VINCENTE MINNELLI: *THE BAD AND THE BEAUTIFUL* (1952)

GREGORY PECK It was a time when the producer was the key figure. The instigator, the galvanizer, the head honcho, was the producer. He chose the director that he thought would be right for the material which he had acquired—novel, play, original, whatever—and then he would "cast" the director. That was pretty much the system when I first came into the business.

MARTIN SCORSESE The making of *Duel in the Sun* is a fascinating example of this. Even an old master like King Vidor, who practically put Hollywood on the map, was not necessarily calling the shots. The major creative force on the film was the producer, David O. Selznick, an

The Crowd (1928): James Murray in King Vidor's unusual pre-Depression drama.

obsessive perfectionist who wanted to top his greatest achievement, *Gone with the Wind*, made seven years earlier.

GREGORY PECK The result was a kind of grandiose quality. It was a bit over the top. Take the barroom scene. There never was such a bar in the West. It was about the size of Madison Square Garden, and almost Oriental in its lavishness.

But to David it was great fun to exaggerate, to heighten. He was having the time of his life. His all-encompassing enthusiasm galvanized everybody. That energy, that sense of playfulness, of rascality—that was Selznick. About one o'clock or two o'clock in the morning, when the actors had to go to sleep, David would settle down and rewrite the script. And we'd get different colored pages the next morning. That didn't always sit well with the directors, but it was David's picture. It was his baby and things were done his way.

The great King Vidor was directing, but David was overcome by his own enthusiasm at times and began more and more to direct over King's shoulder. And that created considerable tension on the set, finally leading to the moment when King stood up somewhere out in Tucson and told David that he knew what he could do with the picture and walked off. William Dieterle finished the picture.

MARTIN SCORSESE Somehow, Vidor survived as an on-again, off-again team player. He even worked again later on with Selznick in television. Vidor was probably the most resilient of the film pioneers—one of the few who were able, time and again, to convince the moguls to let them experiment with the medium. Throughout his career, he succeeded in alternating studio assignments—pictures like *The Champ* and *Stella*

Dallas, with personal projects like *Hallelujah*, *Our Daily Bread* and *The Crowd* (page 22), a most unusual pre-Depression drama. MGM's Irving Thalberg agreed to finance *The Crowd* because Vidor had given the studio its greatest success of the silent era, *The Big Parade*. Sometimes to get his movies produced, Vidor was even willing to mortgage his house or gamble his own salary. Somehow *he* found a way to make one for the studios, one for himself.

The Hollywood of the classical era—the thirties and forties—was based on a powerful, vertically integrated industry. The studios, particularly the five "majors" (MGM, Warner Bros., Paramount, RKO, and Fox) controlled every phase of the process: production, distribution, even exhibition as they owned their own chains of theaters worldwide. To produce fifty pictures a year, each studio held its stars, writers, directors, producers, and an army of skilled technicians, under long-term contracts. They even cultivated a recognizable style, a certain "look" in their films.

GREGORY PECK MGM was more of a dream world, where everything was idealized and somewhat sentimentalized. That came, I think, from L. B. Mayer—what he thought was classy. And Fox leaned more toward, I wouldn't say exactly gritty realism because they made Betty Grable musicals, ice skating pictures, and all kinds of pictures, but toward the things that Zanuck is remembered for—pictures with a social conscience done with a degree of realism. This would probably not be characteristic of MGM.

BILLY WILDER In those days I could look at a picture and if everything was in white silk— MGM! I could look at a picture and if it was Fred

Duel in the Sun (1946): Gregory Peck and Lionel Barrymore look incredulous at producer David Selznick's latest idea.

The Studio Look: In Hollywood's golden era, each studio had an identifiable style. *Camille* (left) shows MGM's idealized world; *Public Enemy* (top), the gritty look of Warner Bros.; and *The Grapes of Wrath* (bottom) is an example of the "social conscience" at Fox.

Astaire—RKO, subsequently MGM. Paramount was a little bit all over the place. They did have their own handwriting with Bing Crosby and Bob Hope, or Martin and Lewis . . . We knew exactly. We went to the same restaurants; we had our own circle. Today, studios don't exist anymore. Sure, you can go in and shoot there, but you move in like you move into the Ramada Inn. You finish shooting, you finish cutting, and it's "Goodbye Charlie."

It's no fun anymore. Not the real fun which we had. Paramount made fifty pictures a year, and even if a picture failed, you went on and on, because to the bosses you were as good as the best thing you had ever done.

MARTIN SCORSESE If you worked at MGM, you had to adjust to the MGM style and it was quite different from the Warner Bros. or the Paramount style. If they did not conform to the studio "look," the mavericks were reined in. Some, like Erich von Stroheim, simply refused to be harnessed and paid a heavy price for it. Buster Keaton, who was very free-wheeling, agonized when MGM put him under the yoke of their supervising producers; his genius didn't survive the treatment.

On the other hand, those who could work comfortably within the system thrived. And they came to define their studio's style: Clarence Brown at MGM, Henry King at Fox, Raoul Walsh at Warner Bros. They were Hollywood pros who rose from the ranks. Most of their long careers were spent under one roof. Michael Curtiz, for example, made no less than 85 films for Warner Bros.—*Casablanca* was his 63rd! That's an average of three features a year, over a period of 28 years. Think of the incredible opportunities directors were given to learn their trade and become true professionals.

There were also talents who needed the discipline of the system to blossom. A perfect example was Vincente Minnelli. He knew, and often acknowledged, that the producer-director dynamic was crucial to the quality and success of a picture. An avant-garde Broadway choreographer, he was lured to Hollywood by producer Arthur Freed and became MGM's resident artist. For thirty years, thanks to sympathetic producers like Freed and later John Houseman, Minnelli had all of the studio's resources at his disposal. The cameras were his brushes and the sound stages his canvas.

All that he loved and hated about Hollywood was distilled in the harsh story of *The Bad and the Beautiful*: the ambition, the power, the opportunism, and the betrayal. No one was spared in the moviemaking process, not even the director. Barry Sullivan's face is unforgettable when he hears from his ruthless partner, played by Kirk Douglas, what has become of their dream project. Incidentally, Kirk Douglas's character was loosely based on several actual producers, among them David O. Selznick.

SCENE: **THE BETRAYAL**

Fred Amiel (Barry Sullivan), who has been pacing back and forth in the anteroom, sees Jonathan Shields (Kirk Douglas) come out of the studio head's office after a long meeting. He can't wait to hear the news. Shields is beaming, but first makes sure he can't be heard by the studio head. He closes the door and takes a deep breath.

Fred Amiel: Well, what happened? Did he go for Gaucho?

Jonathan Shields: Go for him? He had a hemorrhage! "The Far Away Mountains" is gonna be done just the way we want. A million dollar budget!

Amiel *(jumping for joy):* We . . .

The Name above the Title: Director Frank Capra believed in "one man, one film."

Shields: Location in Vera Cruz! Von Ellstein to direct! . . . and Gaucho! Wendy for the girl. Hans Chapman for my cameraman.

Amiel *(in shock)*: Von Ellstein to direct?

Shields: Oh, you're taken care of. Harry agreed. It won't be a separate panel, but your name'll be on the screen: Assistant to the producer.

Amiel: Thanks.

Shields: Oh, Fred, you know this story better than anyone else. It's your baby. Look, I want you with me on the set all the time. You don't have to talk to von Ellstein. Any ideas you have you tell me and I'll tell him.

Amiel: Thanks again. Von Ellstein to direct . . .

Shields: You always said he was the best in the business.

Amiel: Sure he is.

Shields: Fred, I'd rather hurt you now than kill you off forever. You're just not ready to direct a million dollar picture.

Amiel: But you're ready to produce a million dollar picture.

Jonathan Shields *(in close shot)*: With von Ellstein, I am.

VINCENTE MINNELLI: *THE BAD AND THE BEAUTIFUL* (1952)

MARTIN SCORSESE To survive, to master the creative process, each filmmaker had to develop his own strategy. Some, like Frank Capra, Cecil B. De Mille, or Alfred Hitchcock carved a niche for themselves by excelling in a certain type of story and being identified with it. Their very name became a box-office draw. A few even achieved Capra's dream and secured their name "above the title."

FRANK CAPRA (1979) They had wonderful directors at MGM, but you didn't know who they were. You never heard their name. But you heard about me. I made my own film and everybody knew it.

I was the enemy of the major studio. I believed in one man, one film. I believed that one man should make the film and I believed that the director should be that man. One man should do it—I don't give a damn who—but the director has the most to do with it. I just couldn't accept art as a committee. I could only accept art as an extension of an individual.

2

THE DIRECTOR

AS STORYTELLER

James Cagney in Lloyd Bacon's *Footlight Parade.*

MARTIN SCORSESE "If you haven't got the story, you haven't got anything!" Raoul Walsh used to say. This is a cardinal rule in moviemaking. The American filmmaker has always been more interested in creating fiction than in revealing reality. Early on, the documentary form was discarded or relegated to marginal status. For better or for worse, the Hollywood director is an entertainer; he is in the business of telling stories. He is therefore saddled with conventions and stereotypes, formulas and clichés, limitations which were codified in specific genres. This was the very foundation of the studio system.

Audiences loved genre pictures and the old masters never seemed reluctant to supply them. When John Ford rose in the middle of a tempestuous meeting at the Directors Guild of America in 1950, this is how he introduced himself: "My name is John Ford. I make Westerns." He was not referring to his more honored pictures such as *The Informer* or *The Grapes of Wrath*, *How Green Was My Valley* or *The Quiet Man*. His Westerns were what he was most proud of—or so he may have wanted us to believe.

Eventually, film genres would serve to organize assembly-line production: each studio made so many Westerns, so many musicals, and so many gangster films. It all started with Edwin Porter's *The Great Train Robbery*. This was one of the first attempts at scripting a story. Fittingly, it also was a Western.

The first master storyteller of the American screen was D. W. Griffith. His sensibility was steeped in a literary tradition, that of Dickens and Tolstoy, Frank Norris and Walt Whitman. Yet while borrowing from 19th century literature, Griffith was forging the new art of the 20th century. He explored the emotional impact of film and before the outbreak of World War I had

The Great Train Robbery (1903): Edwin S. Porter's Western was one of the first attempts at scripting a story.

already delineated nearly every genre, even the gangster film with his short *The Musketeers of Pig Alley*.

Genres were never rigid. Creative filmmakers kept stretching their boundaries. This was a classical art where personal expression was stimulated rather than inhibited by discipline. Take Raoul Walsh, the most gifted apprentice and disciple of Griffith. His strongest films were variations on a few themes and characters. The figure of the sympathetic outlaw, for instance, a rebel in the tradition of Jesse James, inspired him time and again. In *High Sierra*, you didn't root for the police and the ordinary citizens. You rooted for the gangster. And you knew he was doomed when he became separated from the only person who cared about him, his tarnished angel, Ida Lupino.

At the end of his memoirs, Walsh quoted Shakespeare, his constant inspiration: "Each man in his time plays many parts." This applies not only to Walsh himself, but also to his explosive characters. These outcasts were bigger than life. They stood beyond good and evil. Their lust for life was insatiable, even as their actions precipitated their tragic destiny. The world was too small for them and Walsh often gave them a cosmic battleground: Mount Whitney and the High Sierras.

Eight years after *High Sierra*, Walsh filmed *Colorado Territory*, the same story as a Western. Again he provided his desperado with a wide landscape which dwarfed human figures, this time the City of the Moon and the Canyon of Death. So dear to Walsh's heart was his heroine, now a half-breed outcast, that he gave her as much strength and character as the hero.

You might even sense a mystical dimension at the end of the film that clearly transcended any genre limitation. The lost city is like a primitive cathedral and as he listens to the Navajos chanting in the night, Joel McCrea reflects on his fate and appears to accept it. Walsh used some of the same camera angles as in *High Sierra*. But this time the messenger of death was a Navajo sharpshooter. And in *Colorado Territory*, the tragedy was complete: both protagonists were doomed.

The most interesting of the classic movie genres to me are the indigenous ones: the Western, which was born on the Frontier, the Gangster Film, which originated in the East Coast cities, and the Musical, which was spawned by Broadway. They remind me of jazz: they allowed for endless, increasingly complex, sometimes perverse variations. When these variations were played by the masters, they reflected the changing times; they gave you fascinating insights into American culture and the American psyche.

Walsh's Sympathetic Outlaws and Strong Heroines:
Humphrey Bogart and Ida Lupino in *High Sierra* (top) and
Joel McCrea and Virginia Mayo in *Colorado Territory* (bottom).

The Savage Violence of the Western:
Robert Ryan and Janet Leigh in Anthony Mann's *The Naked Spur*

The Western

MARTIN SCORSESE You can see how a genre evolved just by watching three Westerns John Ford directed with the same actor, John Wayne. The character of the hero becomes richer, more complex, with each decade.

The Ringo Kid of *Stagecoach* (1939) grows first into the benevolent father figure of *She Wore a Yellow Ribbon* (1949). Then Ford transforms him into Ethan Edwards, the misfit of *The Searchers* (1956), who returns from years of wandering to discover that his loved ones have been massacred by the Indians. John Wayne's heroic "persona" has turned dark and obsessive. The physical death of the Indian is not enough. Ethan wants to ensure his spiritual death as well.

SCENE: **A SPIRITUAL DEATH**

The Reverend (Ward Bond) and his posse have found the burial site of a Comanche. With the help of Charlie (Ken Curtis), the Reverend removes the flat boulder and reveals the corpse in a shallow grave. A hand removes the scarf that covers the Indian's face. Ethan Edwards (John Wayne) remains on his horse, at a distance.

Charlie: This one has come a long way before he died, Captain.

Reverend *(to Ethan)*: Well, Ethan, there's another one you can score up for your brother.

(Overcome by grief, young Brad Jorgensen played by Harry Carey, Jr. smashes a large rock into the grave.)

Reverend: Jorgensen!

Ethan *(pulling his gun)*: Why don't you finish the job?

(He fires at the dead Comanche off-screen. Then he fires a second shot.)

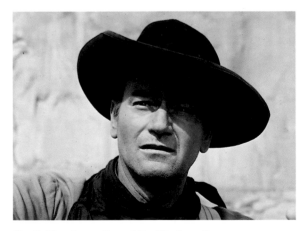

Ford's Transformation of the Western Hero:
John Wayne as a cocky kid in *Stagecoach* (top), a kindly father figure in *She Wore a Yellow Ribbon* (middle), and an obsessive misfit in *The Searchers.*

Mann's Psychological Dramas: The West as a land of greed and vengeance: Gilbert Rowland about to be hanged in *The Furies* (above), and James Stewart reeling in the dead Robert Ryan in *The Naked Spur* (right).

Reverend *(puzzled):* What good did that do ya?
Ethan: By what you preach, none. By what that Comanche believes . . . *(Mose, the Indian scout, points to his own eyes as Ethan speaks)* ain't got no eyes, he can't enter the spirit land—has to wander forever between the winds. You get it, Reverend? *(turning to Martin, the adopted son of Ethan's brother and a boy with Cherokee blood)* Come on, blanket-head.
(Ethan and Martin will pursue the search alone.)
JOHN FORD: *THE SEARCHERS* (1956)

MARTIN SCORSESE Gone is the simple, black and white morality of the early days. Gone are the old-fashioned values of the seasoned Cavalry officer. Ethan Edwards is played by the same star, John Wayne. It is the same location, around Monument Valley, and the same director. But a different character, different attitudes, different conflicts—almost a different country!

Ethan Edwards is actually the most frightening character in the film. He hunts down his niece, who was abducted and raised by the Indians after the massacre of her parents, because he believes she has been "tarnished." "Living with Comanches," he insists, "is not being alive!" After years of searching, when he finally finds her, you don't know whether he is going to kill her or save her. Don't expect a happy ending. There is no home, no family, waiting for Ethan. He is cursed, just as he cursed the dead Comanche. He is a drifter doomed to wander between the winds (page 38).

The Western also allowed for elaborate psychological—and even "Freudian"—dramas. While John Ford only alluded to the dark side, Anthony Mann dwelled in it. In Mann's *The Furies* (1950), the patriarchal cattle baron wants his rebellious daughter to beg him for her lover's life. The proud Mexican lover chooses to die rather than allow his woman to humiliate herself.

The Furies could have been a Greek tragedy. Its powerful story—written by Niven Busch, the author of *Duel in the Sun*—was actually inspired by Dostoevsky's novel, *The Idiot*. The mythology of the Frontier, of a land in perpetual expansion, had given way to greed, vengeance, megalomania, sadistic violence.

SCENE: **IN DOSTOEVSKY'S FOOTSTEPS**

Sitting on his horse, cattle baron Temple C. Jefffords (Walter Huston) observes his daughter Vance (Barbara Stanwyck) running to her lover Juan (Gilbert Roland) who has been captured by the posse. Relishing his role, El Tigre (Thomas Gomez) is preparing the rope.

Juan *(on his knees. He is praying in Spanish and kisses the medal he wears around the neck)*: Amen.

(After signing himself, he stands up and walks toward the noose. El Tigre smiles, looking forward to the execution. Vance runs down the hill. She kisses Juan, laying her hand on his shoulder.)

Juan: The kiss of a good friend.

Vance Jeffords: Till our eyes next meet.

Juan: Till then.

(She embraces him one last time, mounts her horse and rides to the top of the hill where her father sits motionless. El Tigre removes Juan's hat to place the noose around his neck.)

Temple Jeffords *(to his daughter)*: Tears a body to see someone you love hurt, doesn't it?

Vance: Do you want me to beg? Do you want me on my knees to you for his life?

Temple: I'd hang him anyway.

Vance: That's what he said.

Temple: He did, eh? He always was smart.

Vance *(in close shot)*: But you're not! You're old and you're getting foolish and you've made a mistake. It's

me you should have hung! Because now I hate you in a way I didn't know a human could hate. Take a good long look at me, T.C.! You won't see me again until the day I take your world away from you!

(She whips her horse as the noose is tightened around Juan's neck. A Mexican woman is praying on her knees. As the camera pans on Vance who starts riding away from the scene, we hear the cry of anguish.)

Juan's mother: Juanito! Juanito!

(Vance stops her horse. Framed by a huge cactus, she turns to look back. A blood-curling scream is heard.)

Juan's mother: Juanito!!!

ANTHONY MANN: *THE FURIES* (1950)

MARTIN SCORSESE Anthony Mann's brooding heroes were no saints. Seeking revenge was their obsession—an obsession that would consume and nearly destroy them. Even James Stewart, the all-American hero of Frank Capra's fables, succumbed to outbursts of savage violence. In *The Naked Spur* (1953), you see Stewart reel in Robert Ryan, his dead prey. He has become a bounty hunter in order to buy back the ranch stolen from him while he was away fighting in the Civil War.

SCENE: **BITTER TRUTHS**

Howard Kemp (James Stewart) pulls in the body of a wanted man (Robert Ryan). Roy (Ralph Meeker), a renegade officer, has just drowned trying to get to the body in the treacherous white waters. Lina (Janet Leigh) watches, horrified by Howard's determination.

Lina: Cut him loose, Howie!

Howard Kemp *(reeling the body out of the water)*: I'm takin' him back. This is what I came after and now I've got it! No partners, like I said. He's gonna pay for my land.

(Howard drags the body across a flat boulder. Like a dead fish.)

No Happy Ending:
John Wayne, in John Ford's *The Searchers*,
is doomed to a life of homelessness.

Lina: He'll never be dead for you!

Howard (*his back to the camera*): I don't care anything about that. The money, that's all I care about, that's all I've ever cared about. Roy, he called the current, he said face up to it. All right, that's what I'm doing, that's what I'm doing! (*He straddles the body across his horse, behind the saddle.*) Maybe I don't fit your ideas of me, but that's the way I am.

ANTHONY MANN: *THE NAKED SPUR* (1953)

MARTIN SCORSESE Budd Boetticher explored the bare essentials of the Western. His style was as simple as his impassive heroes—deceptively simple. The archetypes of the genre were distilled to the point of abstraction. Bullfighting had been Boetticher's first vocation. The choreography of basic human passions was his forte. In the seven Westerns he made with Randolph Scott, Boetticher always gave precedence to character over action. Each adventure was a poker game and the players' complex moves were more important than the avowed goal. In the power play, the hero and the villain were complementary figures: they shared the same loneliness, the same dreams and even the same ethical code. Somehow the gentleman and the desperado were fascinated by each other.

SCENE: **THE GENTLEMAN AND THE DESPERADO**
At the outlaws' camp, a captive Brennan (Randolph Scott) bumps his head against the roof of the cabin. For a while Frank (Richard Boone) can't stop laughing, but invites him to approach the camp-fire.

Frank: Pour yourself a cup of coffee. Have a seat. Over there. (*Brennan sits down on a log*) You got a wife up on your place?

Brennan: No.

Frank: Should have. Ain't right for a man to be alone.

Brennan: They say that.

Frank: Well, I ought to know.

Brennan: You cook good coffee.

Frank (*gesturing with his gun*): Brennan, talk.

Brennan: What about?

Frank: Your place. What's it like?

Brennan: It's not much, not yet anyway.

Frank: You got stock?

Brennan: Some.

Frank: You work the ground?

Brennan: I plan to. Yeah.

Frank (*smiling*): I'm gonna have me a place someday. I've thought about it, I've thought about it a lot.

Brennan: You figure you'll get it this way?

Frank: Well, sometimes, you don't have a choice.

Brennan: Don't ya?

Frank (*waving his gun*): Now look, Brennan.

BUDD BOETTICHER: *THE TALL T* (1957)

MARTIN SCORSESE For decades, the Western genre embellished the reality of the West to make it more "interesting." But in the mid-fifties, several films started questioning the myth perpetuated by Hollywood. Arthur Penn, in *The Left-Handed Gun* (page 42), for instance, presented Billy the Kid as a juvenile delinquent in search of a father figure. By having a journalist follow the young misfit through his career of crime, Penn suggested how history was distorted even as it was unfolding. Paul Newman portrayed Billy as a suicidal antihero who sought his own death. Neither a vicious killer nor a sympathetic outlaw, Billy was a rebel without a cause. His rage and confusion had more to do with the malaise of adolescents growing up in the 1950s than with the realities of the old West.

ARTHUR PENN We were doing just what they just did again in *Unforgiven*, which is we had a man representing the kind of journalism that was

The Tall T (1957): Boetticher's style is as deceptively simple as his impassive heroes (Randolph Scott, right).

The Left-Handed Gun (1958): Arthur Penn shows the historical distortion of the West by presenting Billy the Kid (Paul Newman) as a suicidal anti-hero.

being produced in the East while the Westerns were really happening. The journalist played by Hurd Hatfield came to believe that the myth he had created was real. So when he went West to meet Billy, he was disappointed because Billy didn't have the kind of heroic, mythic attitudes that he had been attributing to him. Eventually, he became the character that betrayed Billy to Pat Garrett. Their relationship had the aspect of a love affair. In a scene that was unfortunately cut out of the film by the studio, you saw Hatfield being pushed away by Billy, going into a bar and weeping uncontrollably, like a man who has had a love affair broken up.

CLINT EASTWOOD Just when you think that the Western has been exhausted, that there's nowhere else to go with it, there's something that will come along with a new slant on things. It's very exciting when that happens.

In a Western you can get across things that concern you sociologically today. I remember the genre changing, even in the forties with John Wayne and Gary Cooper. Look at Wellman's *The*

Unforgiven (1992): Haunted by his past, gunslinger Munny (Clint Eastwood) settles his accounts with the sheriff who tortured his friend to death.

Oxbow Incident, which analyzed mob violence: it was not successful commercially, but it was a tremendously important film. I guess *High Noon* could have been called "revisionist" in its day. The Western went through sort of "dog days" in the late fifties and then came Sergio Leone, who took a more contemporary and more operatic approach, which was an interesting adventure in the mid-sixties. I tried to take it back to its roots with *Outlaw Josey Wales* and also *Unforgiven*, except that *Unforgiven* does burst the bubble of the myth a little bit.

Unforgiven is a good example of what I mean when you can address a situation. There is a lot of concern in society today about violence and gunplay and that film, even though it takes place in 1880, addresses that now. When you are a perpetrator of violence, and when you get involved in that sort of thing, you rob your soul as well as the person you are committing a violent act against.

MARTIN SCORSESE In *Unforgiven*, Clint Eastwood plays a professional killer who has tried to reform and become a farmer. Physically and mentally scarred, he is haunted by his dark and violent past. Judgment night comes after his best friend has been tortured to death by sheriff Gene Hackman. There is no glamor in killing anymore. The lawman behaves as badly as the renegade. They are both former gunslingers who shot people in the back or when they were unarmed.

SCENE: **JUDGMENT NIGHT**

Munny (Clint Eastwood) enters the brothel where the sheriff (Gene Hackman) tortured his friend (Morgan Freeman) to death. The body is in an open casket in the window. Rain and thunder can be heard throughout.

Munny *(pointing a shotgun at the group)*: Who's the fella owns this shithole?

Bartender: I own this establishment. Bought it from Greely for a thousand dollars.

Munny *(to the rest of the group)*: You better clear out of there.

Bartender: Yes, sir.

Sheriff *(gesturing)*: Just hold it right there. Hold it!

(Munny fires at the bartender who falls backward, killed instantly. On the stairs, prostitutes scream and scatter. Munny then takes aim at the sheriff.)

Sheriff: Well, sir, you are a cowardly son-of-a-bitch. You just shot an unarmed man.

Munny: Well, he should've armed himself if he's gonna decorate his saloon with my friend.

Sheriff: You'd be William Munny out in Missouri. Killed women and children.

Munny: That's right. I've killed women and children. Killed just about everything who walks or crawled at one time or another. And I'm here to kill you, Little Bill. For what you did to Ned. You boys better move away.

CLINT EASTWOOD: *UNFORGIVEN* (1992)

CLINT EASTWOOD I have always felt that the Western movie is one of the few art forms that Americans can lay claim to. Next to jazz.

Americans are somewhat masochistic, I must say, about that. Because sometimes they can be very blasé about their own art forms. The grass is always greener, you know. It's easy to look elsewhere when sometimes great art can be right in front of you.

MARTIN SCORSESE Of course most American directors never claimed to be artists. They prided themselves on appearing blasé. Holding one's cards close to the vest was a survival strategy. Even an old master like John Ford had to wear a mask. He probably enjoyed playing the tight-lipped pro in front of Peter Bogdanovich's camera in this now famous 1971 interview.

SCENE: **KEEPING HIS CARDS CLOSE TO THE VEST**

Ford is interviewed by Bogdanovich against the background of Monument Valley.

Clapper loader *(off camera)*: Eleven, take one.

John Ford: Take one? It won't take more than one take, will it? Shoot.

Peter Bogdanovich *(off camera)*: Mr. Ford, I've noticed that your view of the West has become increasingly sad and melancholy over the years. Comparing for instance *Wagon Master* to *The Man Who Shot Liberty Valance*, have you been aware of that change in mood?

Ford: No. No.

Bogdanovich: Now that I pointed that out, is there anything you'd like to say about it?

Ford: I don't know what you're talking about.

Bogdanovich: Can I ask you what particular element about the Western appealed to you from the beginning?

Ford: I wouldn't know.

Bogdanovich: Would you agree that the point of *Fort Apache* was that the tradition of the Army was more important than one individual?

Ford: Cut!

PETER BOGDANOVICH: *DIRECTED BY JOHN FORD* (1971)

The Tight-lipped Pro: John Ford on the set of his last movie, *7 Women,* with cinematographer Joseph La Shelle.

On the Mean Streets of the Gangster Film:
William A. Sheer in Raoul Walsh's *Regeneration*.

The Gangster Film

The Musketeers of Pig Alley (1912): Movies before WWI portrayed gangsters as products of deprived homes.

MARTIN SCORSESE The Gangster Film—another rich genre which allowed filmmakers to dwell on America's fascination with violence and lawlessness. "There's action only if there is danger." This was said by Howard Hawks, who was an authority on both the Western and the Gangster Film. "To stay alive or die: this is our greatest drama."

The Gangster Film predates World War I with such films as D. W. Griffith's *The Musketeers of Pig Alley* or Raoul Walsh's *Regeneration*, which was shot on location, on New York's Lower East Side. Gangsters then were viewed as the victims of a depressed environment, neighborhood kids growing up on the "mean streets."

But ten years later, Prohibition brought about a tide of movies that signaled a tremendous escalation in urban violence. What struck me in *Scarface* (page 50) was Howard Hawks's cool and distant objectivity. He showed Tony Camonte, also known as Al Capone, as a vicious, immature, irresponsible character. Yet the gangster world was almost attractive because of its irresponsibility. And that was disturbing! At times, of course, the film is very funny. This is not surprising as Hawks was as much a master of comedy as a master of action.

At the end of the thirties came a really pivotal film, Raoul Walsh's *Roaring Twenties*. This chronicle of the Prohibition era was the last great gangster film before the advent of film noir. It read like a twisted Horatio Alger story. The gangster caricatured the American dream.

It was the gripping saga of a war hero turned bootlegger and his downfall after the stock market crash. The gangster had become a tragic figure. Walsh even dared to end the film on a semireligious image that evokes a "Pietà" (page 48). It was actually the inspiration behind one of my student films, *It's Not Just You, Murray*. And I would like to think that *GoodFellas* comes out of the extraordinary tradition spawned by *Scarface* and *The Roaring Twenties*.

SCENE: "HE USED TO BE A BIG SHOT."
Eddie Bartlett (James Cagney) falls on his back on the church steps. They are partially covered with snow. Running behind him is Panama Smith (Gladys George). When she reaches him, it's too late. She holds his head in her arms. A burly cop arrives at the scene and starts questioning her.
Cop: Who is that guy?

47

The Roaring Twenties (1939):
Gladys George cradling the dying
James Cagney in this semireligious
image at the end of Walsh's movie.

Scarface (1932): Prohibition brought a different breed of vicious gangsters to the movies.
Hawks dared to present them (Paul Muni, center) as dangerously attractive.

Panama Smith (*in close shot*)**:** This is Eddie Bartlett
Cop (*in close shot*)**:** What is his business?
Panama Smith: He used to be a big shot.
The camera pulls back to reveal the whole scene: as
the cop takes notes in his pad, Panama cradles in her
hands the head of her dead companion.
RAOUL WALSH: *THE ROARING TWENTIES* (1939)

MARTIN SCORSESE After World War II, the
gangster turned into a businessman. The gang
was taken over by anonymous corporations. The

first film to show these major changes in the
underworld was Byron Haskin's underrated *I
Walk Alone.* I particularly like the scene where
Burt Lancaster, just out of prison, discovers the
new world he's in.

SCENE: **THE NEW DEAL**
Frankie Madison (Burt Lancaster) returns from jail
to claim his share. He confronts Dink Turner (Kirk
Douglas), his former partner in bootlegging, who has
built an empire for himself while Frankie was taking

I Walk Alone (1948): Burt Lancaster (left) confronts his brother (Wendell Corey, center) and former partner (Kirk Douglas, right), who have turned crime into big business.

the rap for their crime.

Frankie *(angry)*: There's only one way to handle you.

Dink *(unimpressed)*: Kill me?

Frankie: If I have to, yeah! A guy's got to fight for what's his.

(Frankie sees the accountant enter with the books: it is his brother Dave played by Wendell Corey).

Frankie: Get him out of here.

Dink: He knows all my business. He stays. This isn't the Four Kings, no hiding out behind a steel door and a peep-hole. This is big business. We deal with banks,

lawyers and a Dun & Bradstreet rating. The world's gone right past you, Frankie. In the twenties, you were great. In the thirties, you might've made the switch. But today you're finished. As dead as the headlines the day you went into prison.

(Later Frankie loses patience as the accountant recites the names of the various corporations set up by the syndicate.)

Accountant: . . . Reeds and Associates . . .

Frankie *(Flicking aside Dave's pen)*: Stop tryin' to dizzy me up. Here *(taking another pen from Dink's*

A Landscape of Moral Conflicts: John Garfield in *Force of Evil*.

breast-pocket), now, I want simple answers. Dave, no diagrams. Dink's got the full say around here, right?

Accountant: Yes.

Frankie: Okay then . . .

Accountant: Except that it's revocable by a vote of the board of directors of Reeds and Associates.

Frankie: Stop the double talk.

Accountant: I'm sorry, Frankie.

Frankie (exasperated): Just what does Dink own?

Accountant: In which corporation?

(In frustration, Frankie looks up at Dink and turns around, totally perplexed.)

BYRON HASKIN: *I WALK ALONE* (1948)

MARTIN SCORSESE Some films, notably Abraham Polonsky's *Force of Evil* (1948), went even further and painted the whole society as corrupt. The face of John Garfield, a lawyer for the mob, was a landscape of moral conflicts. The social body itself was sick. Polonsky's dialogue was unusually poetic, but what you saw was a world of sleaze and greed imploding before your eyes. The system's violence became the issue rather than individual violence.

SCENE: "DYING WHILE YOU ARE BREATHING"
Sitting down in a New York diner, Leo Morse (Thomas Gomez) faces his accountant Freddie Bauer (Howland Chamberlain).

Leo Morse: I'm glad you called me, Freddie. I'm glad you thought it over to listen to me. To calm down and listen to me so I can help you. *(To waiter)* Coffee.

Freddie Bauer: Please, Mr. Morse, all I want is to quit. That's all. Nothing else. They won't let me quit and I want to quit. I'll die if I don't quit.

Leo Morse: I'm a man with heart trouble. I die almost every day myself. That's the way I live. Silly habit! You know, sometimes you feel as though you're dying here *(he touches his pulse)* and here *(touches his fingers)* and here *(touches his heart)*, you're dying while you are breathing.

(Hearing that a car has pulled in front of the diner, he turns toward the door, still holding his coffee cup.)

Leo Morse *(realizing that he has been betrayed)*: Freddie, what have you done? Freddie! What have you done to me?

(Two of the gangsters pull Leo by the arms.)

Gangster #1: Take it easy, Pop. You won't get hurt.

Gangster #2: You're safe with us, Pop. C'mon, you can't take all night. Stand up and walk! *(As they start dragging him out, Freddy Bauer runs for the exit.)*

Gangster #3: Stop him! *(Freddie is tripped by one of the assailants and falls on his back, losing his glasses.)*

Gangster #3 *(yelling hysterically)*: He knows me. Kill him, kill him, he knows me!

(He seizes a gun from one of his men and aims at the accountant's face. The dying man sees the gangster firing at him point blank. Leo is dragged to the car.)

ABRAHAM POLONSKY: *FORCE OF EVIL* (1948)

Force of Evil (1948): The mob expected its members to sacrifice their families. Thomas Gomez is taken by his brother's criminal associates.

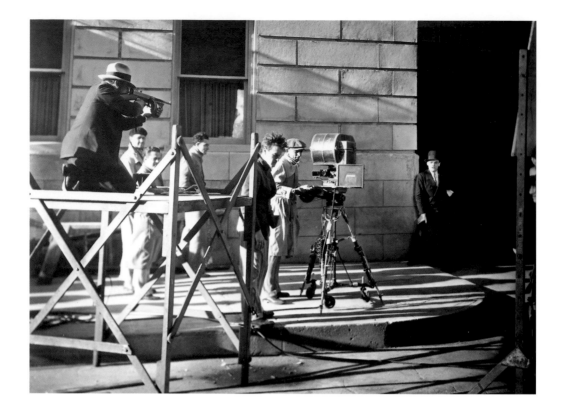

Behind The Scenes: William Wellman directs James Cagney and Edward Woods on the street (left, top) in *Public Enemy*. The finished scenes on film: a machine gun operated by rival gangsters (left, bottom), and Woods being shot (above).

MARTIN SCORSESE You couldn't buck the system; you were indebted to the syndicate for life; they were forever using you. They even wanted you to sacrifice your own family. This madness culminated in Francis Coppola's *The Godfather*. As Al Pacino discovered when he came back from World War II, the son had to follow his father's criminal path. When you were a Corleone, there was no leaving the outfit. It was an evil family bound by fear and torn by treachery, but you served it without ever questioning its legitimacy—as though it was your country. American values—family, free enterprise, patriotism—became totally twisted. Even individualism was dead. The organization was a state within the state; the gangster a chairman of the board; and crime turned into a way of life.

By the late sixties, the gangster genre had proven so versatile that it could even embrace an avant-garde style. In the innovative editing of John Boorman's *Point Blank*, the images are literally flashing through Carroll O'Connor's mind as he realizes who Lee Marvin is—a killer who slugged and smashed his way to the top of the organization in a desperate quest to find the man in charge, the man who can simply pay him.

SCENE: "I WANT MY 93 GRAND!"

Hoping to collect his share of a highjacking operation, Walker (Lee Marvin) waits in ambush inside the villa of one of the organization's leaders, Brewster (Carroll O'Connor). He lets Brewster enter the room and with the butt of his gun smashes the face of the bodyguard carrying the suitcases. This triggers rapid flashes from the past: Walker smashing a bottle in a man's face; Walker pulling down kitchen shelves over another man; Walker hitting a third man's private parts with the butt of his gun. These actions are performed with stunning brutality.

Brewster: Walker! *(Turning to face Walker, pointing an angry finger)* You're a very bad man, Walker! A very destructive man! Why do you run around doing things like this? What do you want?

Walker: I want my money.

(Flashback: Walker threatens to shoot a naked man played by John Vernon whom he is dragging on the floor and who is pulling a sheet around himself.)

Walker's voice-over: I want my 93 grand!

Brewster: $93,000? You threaten a financial structure like this for $93,000? No, Walker, I don't believe you! What do you really want?

Walker: I really want my money.

(Flashback: Walker pushes around a gangster in a business suit, telling him: "I want my money!")

Brewster: Well, I'm not gonna give you any money.

(Flashback: A hand trying to open a package with the butt of a gun.)

Brewster's voice-over: . . . and nobody else is.

Brewster: Don't you understand that?

(Flashback: Walker fires his gun indoors. Carter, one of the syndicate's leaders, tumbles, shot by a sniper in a drainage canal.)

Walker: Well, who runs things?

Brewster: Carter and I run things! I run things!

Walker: What about Fairfax, will he pay me?

Brewster: Fairfax is a man who signs checks.

Walker: No, cash.

Brewster: Cash, checks! Fairfax isn't gonna give you anything, he's finished. Fairfax is dead, he just doesn't know it yet.

Walker: Somebody's got to pay.

JOHN BOORMAN: *POINT BLANK* (1967)

Point Blank (1967): In Boorman's movie, which took on an avant-garde style, this image of Lee Marvin (with Carroll O'Connor) sets up a series of rapid flashbacks.

Musical Drama: James Mason's self-destructive
behaviour in George Cukor's *A Star is Born*

The Musical

MARTIN SCORSESE Parallel to the Gangster Film was the rise of a very different genre: the Musical. This is an interesting coincidence. The harshness of the times, the Depression, colored this most escapist of all film genres.

With choreographer Busby Berkeley the genre came into its own. A former dance instructor, Berkeley was the first to realize that a movie musical was totally different from a staged musical. On film, everything was seen through one eye—the camera. In designing his production numbers, Berkeley would therefore rely on unusual camera movements and angles. The camera itself would partake in the choreography! His ballets could not have existed outside of the movies: they were pure cinematic creations.

Berkeley's films were viewed as pure entertainment, but sometimes he applied his wizardry to the grim realities of American life caught in the grip of the Depression. Always stretching the limits of the musical genre, he even dared to choreograph human tragedies.

Berkeley's early musicals at Warner Bros. offered backstage stories whose pacing was not unlike that of the Gangster Film. They were dominated by the figure of the crazed, manic, often embittered Broadway producer.

In *Footlight Parade* (page 30), you had James Cagney; in *42nd Street* (page 60), Warner Baxter. In those times, if one showed any ambition, one either became a gangster or a show-biz performer—at least in the fantasy world of Warner Bros. Broadway offered a metaphor for a desperate, shattered country. Director or chorus

Meet Me in St. Louis (1944): Minnelli with Judy Garland on the set of this pivotal musical.

girl, your life depended on the show's success. Against all odds, Warner Baxter in *42nd Street* achieved his dream, but on opening night he was too drained to enjoy the production's triumph. The show had taken on a life of its own and the taskmaster's lot in the end was solitude.

Ten years later, Vincente Minnelli's *Meet Me in St. Louis* (page 62) was a milestone. First of all, the story didn't have a Broadway setting; it was a memory album set in the Midwest at the turn of the century. Its protagonists were the members of a middle-class household. They did not need to be professional performers: anyone could sing and dance if they felt like it! Singing and dancing became as natural as breathing or talking.

Also, the tunes were designed to further the plot and reveal the characters. They expressed the ebb

42nd Street (1933): Warner Baxter as the obsessed Broadway producer in
Busby Berkeley's backstage musical, a show-biz figure who burns himself out.

Goldiggers of 1933 (1933): Berkeley realized that a movie musical was different from a staged musical: the camera was part of the choreography in Leroy's movie.

Meet Me in St. Louis (1944): Minnelli's musical was set for the first time in a middle-class household in the Midwest, far from the usual glamourous and frantic world of Broadway.

and flow of personal emotions. Sometimes they were tinged with bittersweet irony as the family faced an uncertain future in the big city. Sweetness and innocence prevailed, but with the explosion of a child's pain and rage, unexpected shadows were suddenly cast on this nostalgic period piece.

SCENE: **PARADISE LOST**

Esther (Judy Garland) tries to console her little sister Tootie (Margaret O'Brien).

Tootie: If Santa Claus brings me any toys, I'm taking them with me. I'm taking all my dolls. The dead ones too. I'm taking everything.

Esther: Of course you are. I'll help you pack them myself. You don't have to leave anything behind. Except your snow people of course.

(Tootie laughs. Outside the snowmen stand in the moonlight. Esther sings: "Have yourself a merry little Christmas. . . . Make the Yule Tide gay. . . . Next years all our troubles will be miles away . . . " At the end of the song, Tootie runs out of the room, down to the garden to decapitate her snowmen. Esther follows her.)

Tootie *(hitting a snowman repeatedly with a stick)*: Nobody's gonna have 'em! Not if we're going to New York! I'd rather kill them if we can't take 'em with us.

My Dream is Yours (1949): In Curtiz's movie, singer Doris Day falls for Lee Bowman, a successful crooner. Their relationship is destroyed when her career takes off.

(The father opens a window on the first floor. From his point of view, we see the two girls in the yard.)
Esther: Tootie, darling, don't cry. You can build other snow people in New York.
Tootie: You can't do anything like you do in St. Louis!
VINCENTE MINNELLI: *MEET ME IN ST. LOUIS* (1944)

MARTIN SCORSESE In the mid-forties, something interesting happened: darker currents seeped into the musical as they had in the Western and the Gangster Film. Even the more conventional musicals hinted at the postwar malaise. On the surface, *My Dream is Yours* had all the trappings of a Doris Day vehicle produced on the Warner Bros. assembly-line. It seemed to be pure escapist fare. But the comedy had a bitter edge. You saw the performers' personal relationships turning sour and being sacrificed to their careers.

Day, an aspiring singer, falls in love with Lee Bowman, a popular crooner, but he's an egotist who feels threatened by his partner's growing success. Significantly, her big break comes when she has to replace him because he is too drunk to perform on his own national radio show. The film makes you aware of how difficult, if not impossible, relationships are between creative people. It

The Bandwagon (1953): Cyd Charisse in Minnelli's satire of Spillane.
This final production number features private eyes and dangerous sirens.

was a major influence on my own musical, *New York, New York*. I took that tormented romance and made it the very subject of the film.

The pinnacle of the musical was reached in the early fifties. MGM was then the magic factory where producer Arthur Freed nurtured such classics as *On the Town*, *An American in Paris*, *Singin' in the Rain*, *It's Always Fair Weather* and, of course, *The Bandwagon*. Again

we meet the incomparable Vincente Minnelli. If you look at *The Bandwagon*'s final production number, "The Girl Hunt Ballet," a satire of Mickey Spillane's pulp novels, you'll see the musical genre borrowing and absorbing the icons of film noir: private eyes and dangerous sirens. Minnelli's musicals celebrated the triumph of the imaginary over the real. Any aspect of reality, however trivial, could be transformed, stylized, and incorporated into a ballet: the world was a stage and it belonged to those who could sing and dance.

George Cukor's *A Star is Born* took the genre one step further. It gave us Judy Garland as a band singer who becomes a movie star while James Mason, her mentor, sabotages his career. Actually, the story had been brought to the screen twice before in a nonmusical form.

"The show must go on" is the performer's first commandment, but Mason's Norman Maine was trapped in the cruel maze of make-believe. He couldn't take it anymore. He couldn't even bear to look at himself. Breaking mirrors (page 58) was his first step towards self-destruction. This was no longer a musical comedy. This was a musical drama about the sad ironies of show-business.

In spite of bold attempts by choreographer-directors Gene Kelly, Stanley Donen, and Bob Fosse to open up new territories, the musical ceased to exist as a film genre. But the show-biz performer remains a key figure in film biographies. Recently, the most exciting effort was probably Bob Fosse's self-portrait, *All That Jazz*. The figure of the exhausted entertainer needing open-heart surgery would fit right into Busby Berkeley's gallery of hard-driving, hard-drinking, chain-smoking directors.

A Star is Born (1954): A jealous James Mason sabotages his own career when his protegée Judy Garland becomes a movie star.

to die. I want to live."
(Gideon mumbles unintelligibly as he is given a shot.)
Director: Well, look. If you can't say it, we'll just have to cut it, that's all. Cut it! Take me up. Next set-up!
(The director is hoisted up on his crane.)
BOB FOSSE: *ALL THAT JAZZ* (1979)

SCENE: **THE SHOW MUST GO ON**
After his heart attack, Joe Gideon played by Roy Scheider is lying on a hospital bed. He can only groan.
Director's voice: Cut!
(Gideon's alter ego appears to him: he's a film director sitting on a Chapman crane, smoking a cigarette.)
Director *(to Gideon)*: You blew it! You forgot your line. At the end of this number, you're supposed to say, uh, what's he supposed to say?
Script supervisor: He's supposed to say, "I don't want

3

THE DIRECTOR

AS ILLUSIONIST

Henry B. Walthall in D.W. Griffith's *The Birth of a Nation*.

MARTIN SCORSESE Of course, it is not enough for the director to be just a storyteller. To implement his vision, he has to be a technician and even an illusionist. This means controlling and mastering the technical process. Our palette has expanded tremendously through a century of constant experimentations as the movies grew from silent to sound, black and white to Technicolor, standard screen size to Cinemascope, 35mm to 70mm. The American movie industry, it seems, never failed to embrace new technological developments. Somehow, it moved faster and more decisively than its foreign rivals.

As King Vidor said, "The cinema is the greatest means of expression ever invented. But it is an illusion more powerful than any other and it should therefore be in the hands of the magicians and wizards who can bring it to life."

Buster Keaton may have had the same thought when he made *The Cameraman*. His character was actually that of an aspiring cameraman. In the hope of getting a job he showed his footage to MGM executives. Unfortunately, he had double-exposed the film: divers were leaping in reverse, a battleship cruised down 5th Avenue, cars and trucks collided in an urban kaleidoscope. . . The screening was a disaster. However, as every director will experience, accidents can be the source of extraordinary poetry and beauty. All that Keaton's cameraman needed was to learn and master the language of film.

Interestingly, most of the early film pioneers, including D. W. Griffith, had no formal education. They were self-taught and often shared the prevailing prejudice that the cinema was a minor form of entertainment. The American film probably came of age in February 1915 when Griffith opened his first feature-length epic, *The Birth of a Nation*.

According to Raoul Walsh, who was one of Griffith's assistants at the time and who played the role of John Wilkes Booth, it took *The Birth of a Nation* to convince Americans that "films were an art in their own right and not just the illegitimate offspring of the theater." How did Griffith achieve this triumph? Essentially through his composition and orchestration of the shots. As Walsh put it: "The high and low angle shots turned a good picture into a great one." One close-up was worth a thousand words. Erich von Stroheim, also one of Griffith's assistants, acknowledged that he was "the pioneer of filmdom, the first to put beauty and poetry into a cheap and tawdry sort of amusement."

I have always felt that visual literacy is just as important as verbal literacy. What the film pioneers were exploring was the medium's specific techniques. In the process, they invented a new language based on images rather than words, a visual grammar you might say: close-ups, irises, dissolves, masking part of the frame for emphasis, dolly shots, tracking shots. These are the basic tools that directors have at their disposal to create and heighten the illusion of reality. When Lillian Gish called D. W. Griffith the father of film, she used the same analogy: "He gave us the grammar of filmmaking. He understood the psychic strength of the lens."

Half a century later, Stanley Kubrick may have had Griffith in mind when he remarked that what is truly original in the art of filmmaking, what distinguishes it from all the other arts, may be the editing process. As a matter of fact, the technique of cross-cutting was developed by Griffith two years before *The Birth of a Nation*. In *Death's Marathon*, for instance, a 1913 short film, he shows you two events happening simultaneously and intercuts them to increase the

The Cameraman (1928): Buster Keaton as a cameraman
learning to master the language of film in Sedgwick's movie.

The Birth of a Nation (1915): Griffith's composition and orchestration of such shots as these featuring Henry B. Walthall (top) and Raoul Walsh playing John Wilkes Booth (bottom) convinced Americans that film was an art in its own right.

suspense. At the time, Griffith had to fight his distributors who feared that audiences would be confused by such an innovation.

It was in the great epics of the silent era that the illusionists learned to use special effects and visual wizardry to conjure up some of their most compelling visions. The American tradition of the great spectacle was born circa 1915, when Griffith saw *Cabiria*, an Italian superproduction. Giovanni Pastrone's *Cabiria* had all the right ingredients: adventure, melodrama, pageantry, religion, extraordinary production design, and striking camera angles and lighting. To film the crossing of the Alps, they actually had to drag Hannibal's elephants up onto a mountain top.

Reportedly, Griffith watched it twice in one night. It inspired him; it gave him the audacity to create his masterpiece, *Intolerance*. Much has been made of the epic production's extravagant budget, real-size sets and thousands of extras. Griffith's achievement is all the more extraordinary because he worked without a script. It was all planned in his head—not on paper. But Griffith went even further in his experiments. *Intolerance* was a daring attempt at interweaving stories and characters, not from the same period, but from four different centuries. Freely cross-cutting from one era to another, he blended them all together in a grand symphony devoted to one idea—a passionate plea for tolerance.

Griffith's passion for history was balanced by his passion for simple people, the victims of history. In the episode set in modern-day America, a young woman is deemed an unfit mother because her husband is in jail (page 72). Oppression is represented by society matrons, puritan Reformers who want to place her baby in an orphanage. Griffith's distressed heroines— Mae Marsh as the Dear One, Constance Talmadge

Cabiria (1914): Giovanni Pastrone's melodramatic spectacle with its grand production design and striking lighting was an influence on Griffith.

Intolerance (1916): With interweaving stories (the St. Bartholomew Massacre, above) from different time periods, Griffith made his grandiose movie without a script.

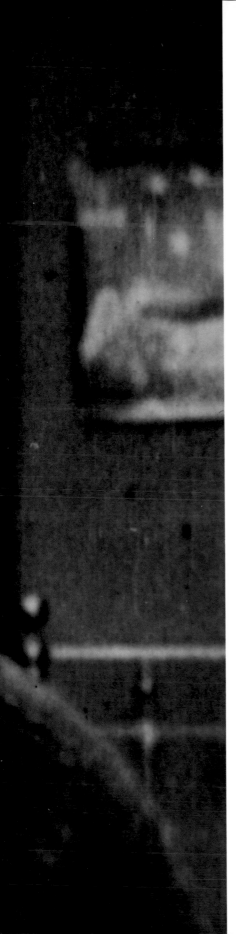

Intolerance (1916): Mae Marsh
in the modern-day American episode
of Griffith's movie, an eloquent close-
up of one of his victims of history.

The Ten Commandments (1923): For this silent version, Cecil B. De Mille insisted that every detail be seen with equal clarity in such scenes as "The Parting of the Red Sea", led here by Theodore Roberts.

as the Mountain Girl, and Margery Wilson as Brown Eyes—carried with them the heart and soul of the picture. For them he composed his most eloquent close-ups.

Like Griffith, Cecil B. De Mille liked to paint on a big canvas. His ambition was "to tell an absorbing story against a background of great historical events." What inspired his first Biblical epic was one simple belief: "You cannot break the Ten Commandments, they will break you!" Most impressive was De Mille's masterful staging of the Exodus from Egypt, the visual contrasts between the Pharaoh's war machine and the loose caravan

of the Israelites, the sense of wonder, the attention to details, even in large crowd scenes. His miniatures were as powerful as his frescoes. He even used an early two-strip Technicolor process. However, the grandiose set pieces were always subordinate to the story. De Mille knew that spectacle alone would never make a great picture. He spent much more time working on dramatic construction than on planning photographic effects. "The audience," he said, " is interested in individuals whom they can love or hate."

De Mille also believed that he could translate the words of the Bible in the language of film—

The Ten Commandments (1956): Edward G. Robinson with the Golden Calf in De Mille's remake of his silent film. With its stunning special effects and colors, and dreamlike images, this movie was a sumptuous visual fantasy.

literally. To achieve this, he devised extraordinary technical effects, such as the parting of the Red Sea. He insisted that every detail be seen with equal clarity. During the parting of the waters, you will notice the rocks and seaweed scattered on the sand to make the beach look like the bottom of the sea. It was a last minute inspiration on the part of De Mille, who led his army of extras into the surf and showed them how to gather the kelp.

Naturally, I never saw De Mille's silent films when I was a boy. His later epics are the ones that made an indelible impression on me, particularly

Samson and Delilah and his own remake of *The Ten Commandments*, which I have seen countless times. De Mille presented such a sumptuous fantasy that if you saw his movies as a child, they stuck with you for life. The marvelous superseded the sacred. What I remember most vividly are the tableaux vivants, the colors, the dreamlike quality of the imagery, and of course the special effects. "God is a unique flame, but the flame is a different color to different people." These were the words of Ramakrishna which De Mille quoted to define his own faith.

The great illusionists of the past, D. W.

Sunrise (1927): Murnau offered visions rather than plot with such images of George O'Brien with Margaret Livingstone as a vamp, the city girl (left, top) who tempted the young farmer to drown his wife Janet Gaynor (left, bottom). Later the broken couple is reunited (above).

Griffith, Cecil B. De Mille, Frank Borzage, King Vidor, were conductors. They orchestrated visual symphonies, what Vidor called "silent music." It would fade away as Hollywood embraced sound, but the legacy of the silent era was remarkable. American movies had matured into a sophisticated art form, with elaborate camera moves, long takes, deep focus, expressive lighting, complex miniatures. In the late twenties, the most exciting experiments were taking place at the Fox studios, where the German master Friedrich Murnau was given carte blanche on the strength of his European triumphs. *Sunrise* (page 76) became the most expensive art film made in Hollywood.

Rather than a plot, Murnau offered visions, a landscape of the mind. His ambition was to paint his characters' desires with lights and shadows. When the frenzied city girl tempted the young farmer, she conjured up a kaleidoscope of images. The vamp wants the young husband to leave everything behind. His land, his wife, his child, the peace and innocence of the country life. After she plants a deadly thought in her lover's mind, Murnau has George O'Brien's shoes weighted with twenty pounds of lead to give the actor a more threatening presence.

Murnau called *Sunrise* "a story of two humans." He said, "This song of the Man and his Wife is of no place. You might hear it anywhere at any time." They do not have a name, but you experience every idea, every emotion they feel.

Murnau was called a cerebral director by his Hollywood peers because he demanded that his actors fully understand the mind of their character: "I talk to an actor of what he should be thinking rather than what he should be doing." The camera, he remarked, is "the director's sketching pencil. It should be as mobile as possible to catch every fleeting mood. It must whirl and peep and move from place to place as swiftly as thought itself."

Later in their journey, the broken couple of *Sunrise* are reunited. Fear and guilt fade away. They become invulnerable. Nothing can harm them anymore—not even the city's hustle and bustle. Magically, subjective perceptions take on an objective reality. A superimposition serves as an inner vision or an inner monologue. What Murnau is projecting onto the environment is their dream, their common dream, at least for a brief moment.

In *Sunrise*, love and death were intertwined like day and night. In Frank Borzage's *Seventh Heaven*, love negated death itself. Both films starred Janet Gaynor, who commuted between the two sets, working with Murnau during the day and with Borzage at night. In Borzage's film she is a street angel. Her savior is Charles Farrell, a streetsweeper. Reluctantly, he takes her to his lofty garret above the city. He works in the sewers of Paris, but insists that he lives near the stars.

Borzage was not a highly educated man, let alone an art historian like Murnau. His approach to the medium was more instinctive. He was a maestro of the pantomime. What inspired him was the sheer power of emotions. This was the great mystery that elevated his melodramas into pure songs of love. Directed by Borzage, Janet Gaynor and Charles Farrell formed a unique couple, at once vibrant with sexual passion and wrapped in a mystical aura. Their romance would lift them from the physical to the spiritual.

War rips them apart, but as Borzage once stated, "Souls are made great through love and adversity." He deeply believed in the transcendent power of love. Even when Farrell is blinded in the trenches, the lovers remain in daily telepathic communication. Time and space can be surmounted and even abolished. Ultimately,

Seventh Heaven (1927): Charles Farrell, a street cleaner, and his angel Janet Gaynor
in his garret high above the city. Borzage's film is one of sheer emotion.

because Gaynor refuses to accept Farrell's death, she is able to bring him back from the dead. For the lovers reality itself is immaterial.

In the late twenties the art of the pantomime had reached its zenith. But the era of sound had arrived and for the silent film directors this was a time of painful transition. Even a script conference called for new skills.

KING VIDOR (1980) We were so imbued and so living in pantomime that a fellow would come in and tell a story to, say, Thalberg at MGM, a comedy story in particular, and he'd tell the whole damn story in pantomime. He comes in and "ahh . . ." and "sock", you know, "hit . . ." Everything was like that. Like cartoon strips.

When sound came in, it was absolutely normal for directors such as René Clair, Clarence Brown, Chaplin, and many others to be against it. They thought they had achieved a medium of expression—that with close-ups and lighting you could show what somebody was thinking. You didn't

Her Man (1930): With fluid camera moves, Garnett skillfully choreographs this fistfight in a honkytonk bar (Ricardo Cortez at center in pin–stripe suit).

Anna Christie (1930): Greta Garbo and director Clarence Brown on the set where the mike, a new invention, over the table will be hidden by a lantern so as not to show on film.

need anything else. That was the whole art of silent films. Then all of a sudden, we're dealing with dialogue. I had, from the time I was 12 or 13, thought entirely in terms of images and pictures and movements. What is an interesting movement? And here we are with words.

MARTIN SCORSESE The studios bowed to the tyranny of sound experts who knew little about filmmaking. At first, they had the cameras enclosed in a soundproof booth or ensconced in a blimp. As William Wellman put it, "Creaking floors received more attention than creaking stories!" Actors were kept anchored within the range of microphones. These had to be hidden, sometimes in rather obvious props, like the barge's lantern in *Anna Christie*.

Traditionally, film historians insisted that at that time movies stopped moving. But the myth of the static camera has been dispelled now that so many films of that period are being rediscovered. There were some who refused to be shackled or paralyzed—directors such as Rouben Mamoulian, Frank Capra, William Wellman, Tay Garnett, all of whom can be credited with getting the camera moving again.

Most Tay Garnett pictures of the early thirties feature fluid camera moves and even very long takes. In *Her Man* (page 80), for instance, you have to admire how skillfully the camera follows a tray with two glasses across the dance floor of a honkytonk bar. The choreography looks effortless, but trust me, long shots like these must have been very hard to achieve.

The dreamlike world of the silent film was no more. A more naturalistic approach seemed to prevail in the talkies. But in fact sound encouraged the illusionist to heighten reality. In George Hill's *The Big House*, the sound effects alone suggest that the convicts are anonymous robots. Then in the chapel, as soon as you hear their voices, they come alive. They are given an identity and a purpose when their actions contradict the chorus of prayer—a very effective counterpoint.

Sound can enhance the drama tremendously, particularly when it depicts an event that you are not shown. In *Scarface*, Howard Hawks demonstrated that sound and visual effects can blend into a deadly metaphor. Sound can also tell the whole story as Wild Bill Wellman proved repeatedly. A poet of stark images and brutal understatements, he loved to jolt, deceive and even frustrate his audience by depriving them of a spectacular scene. In *The Public Enemy*, he dared to stage the film's climax and the hero's comeuppance offscreen.

The Big House (1930): The advent of sound heightened the reality of this prison scene in Hill's movie. The previously anonymous convicts come to life as they pray in the chapel.

Three-strip Technicolor in the mid-thirties, this dramatically improved process was a wonderful gift bestowed on the illusionist. In the old two-strip Technicolor, the one DeMille used in the silent *Ten Commandments*, blue could not be reproduced. Now the three-strip process covered the entire spectrum. Extra-wide cameras could expose three negatives simultaneously, each recording one of the primary colors.

Yet, rather than encouraging realism, the Technicolor palette added flamboyance to the melodrama. Look at Gene Tierney in John Stahl's *Leave Her to Heaven*, an angel face with the darkest of hearts (page 84)! This was a fascinating hybrid: a film noir in color, starring a neurotically possessive woman destroying anybody who might come between her and her husband, even the unwanted child she's carrying. Her husband's younger brother, a paraplegic boy, was in her way too.

Leave Her to Heaven (1945): A film noir in color. The brilliant Technicolor enhanced this melodrama in which Gene Tierney plays a neurotic, possessive woman.

SCENE: **FILM NOIR IN COLOR**

Ellen (Gene Tierney) and Danny, her husband's young paraplegic brother (Darryl Hickman) are canoeing on the lake. She has just told him she's planning a trip with her husband. Without him.

Ellen *(smiling)*: We wouldn't be separated for long. Just a few weeks.

Danny: No, I'd rather wait.

(He lowers himself into the water. Ellen is rowing. She now wears dark sunglasses.)

Ellen: Do you think you can make it, Danny?

Danny: Aah, it's a cinch.

(He swims ahead of the canoe.)

Ellen: Don't worry about your direction now. I'll keep you on your course.

Danny *(swimming)*: Okay!

(He stops, experiencing some difficulty.)

Danny: I, I think I'm getting tired.

Ellen: Take it easy. You don't want to give up when you've come so far.

Danny *(swimming again)*: Okay, I'll get my second wind in a minute . . . *(He stops again.)* Oh, ah, the water's cold, colder than I thought! I, I had too much lunch. I have a stomachache. Aaah! It's, it's a cramp! It's a cramp!!!

(He goes under. Ellen is not rowing anymore. She doesn't make a move. A moment later, in a desperate burst of energy, he reemerges.)

Danny: Ellen, Ellen! Help me!!!

(He drowns. Ellen remains motionless. She seems to be in a trance. She comes out of it and takes off her sunglasses upon hearing her husband Cornel Wilde whistling on the shore. She sees him walking toward their cabin, unaware of the drama.)

Ellen *(rising and pretending to realize that something is terribly wrong)*: Danny, Danny!!!

(As the husband reacts, she takes off her robe and dives into the water.)

JOHN STAHL: *LEAVE HER TO HEAVEN* (1945)

MARTIN SCORSESE You have to remember that color was rarely used for contemporary subjects. It was associated with period pieces and musicals. John Stahl's direction and Leon Shamroy's cinematography conjured up an unsettling super-realist vision. This was a lost paradise, its beauty ravished by the heroine's perverse nature.

The illusionist always knew that color itself can actually play a dramatic role. This is what Nicholas Ray attempted in *Johnny Guitar*, a truly offbeat Western. Joan Crawford was Vienna, the outsider persecuted by the so-called respectable citizens because of her ties to a band of renegades. Ray reversed the genre's traditional iconography. Black was the color of Mercedes McCambridge and the vigilantes, while the outcasts were endowed with rich colors or even pure white.

You can mirror emotions with color. Ray designed and adorned Vienna's gambling house like the set of a baroque opera. Colors were deliberately distorted or thrown off balance. Blue was toned down in favor of deep, saturated colors. When an insane jealousy compels McCambridge to destroy Crawford's palace, the palette alone suggests a fury from hell.

SCENE: **A BAROQUE OPERA**

Vienna (Joan Crawford) is sitting at her piano when Emma (Mercedes McCambridge) and a posse raid the gambling house. They are searching for the Dancing Kid and his friends. Emma has a personal motive: she has been spurned by the Kid who became Vienna's lover. The piano is set on a platform against a background of dark red rock.

Vienna: Are you satisfied they're not here?

Emma *(stepping up)*: No!

(Some of the vigilantes scatter. A few run upstairs. Others cross the hall.)

The Marshal: We came for the Kid and his bunch.

Johnny Guitar (1954): Ray reversed the usual iconography to heighten the emotions. The outcast Joan Crawford (right, with Ben Cooper) is in white, while Mercedes McCambridge (left) and her posse wear black. The scene is set against a vividly colored background.

Vienna *(still playing)*: I'm sitting here in my own house minding my own business, playing my own piano. I don't think you can make a crime out of that. *(The vigilantes have found the wounded Turkey, played by Ben Cooper, hiding under a table and drag him to the center of the scene. The front of the boy's shirt is covered with fresh blood. Vienna reacts.)*

Emma: You're only a boy. We don't want to hurt you. Just tell us she was one of you and you'll go free!

(The Marshal, played by Frank Ferguson, looks extremely uneasy. Another vigilante, McIvers, is played by Ward Bond.)

McIvers: Come on, Turkey, tell us. I'll give you my word you won't hang.

Turkey *(desperate, turns and looks up to Vienna)*: What should I do? I don't want to die. What do I do?

Vienna: Save yourself.

Emma *(barking)*: Well, was she?

(Terrorized, Turkey nods.)

NICHOLAS RAY: *JOHNNY GUITAR* (1954)

MARTIN SCORSESE Now the size of the screen itself needed to grow. It couldn't be contained. In the mid-fifties, it spilled over its boundaries into something much grander. I still remember one of the great experiences I had in my film-going, back in 1953. I was ten or eleven years old. It was at the Roxy Theatre. The curtain began to open, and continued to open, until it revealed the biggest screen I'd ever seen. On it was the first Cinemascope picture, *The Robe.*

Originally, the new aspect ratio was a commercial gimmick designed to give the film industry an edge over its rival, television. Yet many filmmakers

East of Eden (1955): Kazan innovatively uses Cinemascope (see page 191) in this intimate family drama. He combines the old and new proportions by filming narrow doorways and halls in the wider format as James Dean pleads for his mother to speak to him.

resisted the innovation. "It's only good for funerals and snakes!" pronounced Fritz Lang. It was a huge canvas and directors were put to the test as they learned to master the new proportions.

At first, Elia Kazan disliked the format, but *East of Eden* showed that Cinemascope could suit an intimate family drama as well as vast frescoes. You were not limited to landscapes or processions, horizontal lines or diagonal movements. When James Dean in *East of Eden* dares to enter his long-lost mother's bordello for the first time, Kazan is able to play with the configuration of his set. He actually combines the old and the new proportions in his composition, introducing narrower frames such as doorways and corridors within the wide format itself.

Few were as skilled as Vincente Minnelli in using Cinemascope for dramatic effect. In the tragic finale of *Some Came Running*, the actors seem to blend into their surroundings (page 90). The suspense actually derives from their integration in the environment: you don't know if and when the killer and his unsuspecting prey will come together in the same space. Cinemascope allows Minnelli to deploy a more complex, and therefore more threatening image. The more open the frame, the greater the impression of depth, and the more striking the illusion of reality. We are presented with a vibrant, chaotic canvas and it is up to us to explore and interpret it.

SCENE: "'WHOM' IS THE OBJECTIVE."

Parkman, Illinois. As they stroll across a street carnival, Dave Hirsh (Frank Sinatra) and Ginny (Shirley MacLaine) are stalked by Raymond, her former lover (Steven Peck). Ginny, the whore with a big heart, is holding on her arm a fake fox fur.

Ginny: I got one of them... them grammar books from the libary [sic]. I got it from that teacher who—whom

. . . "Whom" is the objective.

Dave: "Whom" says so?

Ginny: Hmmm? *(she laughs)*

(Cut to Raymond running madly. The lights of a merry-go-round circle above his head. Back to Dave and Ginny making their way through the crowd. Cut to Dave's friend Bama, played by Dean Martin, who is running too, trying to prevent the tragedy. Bama appears in the same spot and is framed in the same fashion as Raymond. Still running, Raymond pulls his gun from his suit jacket. He stops a moment to take aim from behind a scaffold. Struck by the first bullet, Dave falls backward. Ginny freezes, tries to identify the killer and pivots as he rushes forward to finish the job. In the process he bumps into people and equipment. As Raymond fires again, Ginny blocks the shot by diving forward and collapsing on Dave's body. Bama arrives too late on the scene. Dave seems to be holding Ginny's inert body in his arms. He raises his hand. It is covered with her blood.)

VINCENTE MINNELLI: *SOME CAME RUNNING* (1958)

MARTIN SCORSESE The impact of the wide screen was particularly significant on such genres as the Western and the Epic. When he started *Land of the Pharaohs* (page 91), Howard Hawks was nervous about the new format. "It's good only for showing great masses in movement," he complained. "It's hard to focus attention and it's very difficult to edit."

However his approach proved masterful. It was the composition of the shots themselves that helped us appreciate the human efforts and technical feats that the filmmakers attributed to the pyramid builders. This was like a documentary made on location in 2800BC. The wide screen gave the sense we were really there. This is the way people lived and worked; this is what they believed, endured, and achieved.

Some Came Running (1958): Minnelli's use of Cinemascope creates a threatening and suspenseful setting for the killer's unsuspecting prey (Shirley MacLaine, in the crowd with Frank Sinatra).

HOWARD HAWKS (1977) I just shot it the way you see a thing. I shoot straightforward too. I resent camera movements that you become conscious of. I don't use any camera tricks. The camera is usually eye height. The audience sees just what we see.

MARTIN SCORSESE Today, a film like *The Fall of the Roman Empire* (page 92) has the poignant beauty of a lost art. For this was the autumn of the great American epics. They simply became too expensive to make. Like Howard Hawks, Anthony

Mann had been a master of the Western. *The Fall of the Roman Empire* offered a multilayered drama which was as intense as *The Naked Spur*, *The Far Country* or *Man of the West*. Mann's sense of space and dramatic composition had never been more evident. Throughout the film, you could hear the gods laugh in the background—a cruel laugh that spelled the doom of all the protagonists and of the Roman Empire.

So, is the grand old tradition started by *Cabiria* and *Intolerance* obsolete? It would seem so. Today, there is no need to drag Hannibal's

The Land of the Pharaohs (1955): Hawks was uncertain about using wide screen but proved masterful at the new format, here realistically recreating life in 2800BC Egypt.

elephants up the Alps anymore; they can be generated by the computer. Is this the end of epic cinema or the dawn of a new art form?

GEORGE LUCAS Nobody can afford to buy three or four thousand extras. It's not economically feasible anymore because you have to costume them, you have to transport them, you have to feed them and you move very slowly when you are trying to direct a large group of people live. Doing that today is next to impossible. But doing it digitally, you get a small group of people, say one

hundred people, and you replicate them and move them around, and you can have exactly the same effect for one-tenth of the cost.

When we started *Jurassic Park*, we had no idea that we could do any of that. We were starting out doing normal puppet animation, like Ray Harryhausen had done. Even the computer artist didn't know we would eventually make a realistic looking dinosaur. It is done now. We have been able to do it with people, with animals, and now in our TV series, *Young Indiana Jones*, with locations. We have been able to replicate, or erase,

The Fall of the Roman Empire (1964): In one of the last great epics, which became too expensive to make, Mann shows a masterful sense of space and dramatic composition.

2001 (1968): Keir Dullea as a young man (right) who, thanks to Stanley Kubrick's magic, is transformed into a wizened body (above) in this experimental and visionary masterpiece.

people, things and places. We have changed the medium in a profound way. It is no longer a photographic medium. It is now a painterly medium and it's very fluid so that things that are in the frame you can take out, move, put them over here. It's almost going from two to three dimensions in the dynamic that has been created at this point.

FRANCIS COPPOLA There is a misconception that we are surrendering something of art to a technology that will do it for us. That is never the case.

But cinema itself is technology and to say that, "Oh well, it can't be an art because it is a mechanical device rushing celluloid through it" is as naive as to say, "You can't create because it is a computer rushing numbers through it." The technology is always an element of creativity, but it never is the source of the creativity and so my attitude is to embrace technology as it comes.

When I was working on *Apocalypse Now*, I realized that there must be another way to make movies other than the arduous mechanical way. I knew that the cinema would become electronic and therefore embrace the techniques of live television. Electronic editing allows you to go through many more creative possibilities which would be too time-consuming in the mechanical mode. You can sketch your wildest ideas and do a lot of the editing yourself. On every film that I have made since, I have been able to try things that pop into my head without other editors and that long expensive process. What that new environ-

ment really means is that the final image you achieve can be what you imagined. Anything you wish to see you are able to create.

BRIAN DE PALMA In any kind of art form, you're creating an illusion for the audience to look at reality through your special eye. The camera lies all the time. It lies twenty-four times a second.

MARTIN SCORSESE In other words, we are all the children of D. W. Griffith and Stanley Kubrick. Take *2001*, the first film to link the camera and the computer in the creation of special effects for the spaceship's journey into the unknown. This was a breakthrough in technical wizardry. Every frame of *2001* made you aware that the possibilities for cinematic manipulations are indeed infinite. Like Griffith's *Intolerance*, like

Murnau's *Sunrise*, it was at once a superproduction, an experimental film and a visionary poem.

Whether the illusion is created through high-tech or low-tech wizardry doesn't really matter. The magic will only be effective if it is carried by a strong vision. And it can be achieved in so many ways. Fifty years ago, when he was assigned to a small B-film called *Cat People*, director Jacques Tourneur had practically no budget and of course none of today's new technologies. But he knew that the dark has a life of its own. Instead of showing the creature who threatened his protagonist, he would only suggest a presence and to do that, he simply conjured up an ominous shadowplay. It was a sleight of hand that an early film magician could have performed at the turn of the century.

4

THE DIRECTOR

AS SMUGGLER

MARTIN SCORSESE We have looked at the rules, at the narrative codes, at the technical tools. And have seen how Hollywood filmmakers adjusted to these limitations; they even played with them. Now is the time to look at the cracks in the system.

What slipped through these cracks has always fascinated me. There were opportunities, there were projects that allowed for the expression of different sensibilities, offbeat themes, or even radical political views—particularly when the financial stakes were minimal. Less money, more freedom! The world of B-films was often freer and more conducive to experimenting and innovating. Directors in the forties found that they could exercise more control on a small budget movie than on a prestigious A-picture. Also, they had fewer executives looking over their shoulder. They could introduce unusual touches, weave unexpected motifs, and sometimes transform routine material into a much more personal expression. In a sense, they became smugglers. They cheated and somehow got away with it.

Style was crucial. The first master of esoterica was Jacques Tourneur, who began making his mark in low-budget supernatural thrillers. On *Cat People*, he had a good reason not to show the creature. "The less you see, the more you believe," he stated. "You must never try to impose your views on the viewer, but rather you must try to let it seep in, little by little." This oblique approach perfectly defines the smuggler's strategy.

The son of pioneer filmmaker Maurice Tourneur, Jacques Tourneur had the good fortune to find an extraordinary oasis of creative subversion in producer Val Lewton's unit at RKO. Lewton, a former story editor for Selznick, was once described as "a benevolent David Selznick." He worked extensively on all of the scripts that he

Master of Esoterica: Jacques Tourneur (left) on the set of *Cat People*.

produced, but he never set foot on the set and left the director to his own devices.

SCENE: **THE UNSEEN**

Walking along a park late at night, Alice (Jane Randolph) appears to be stalked by an unseen presence. She turns to look back, but the street is deserted. She walks faster. A loud hiss makes her jump. It is only a municipal bus pulling up. Yet above her, some branches move ominously.

Bus driver: Climb on, sister. Are you riding with me or ain't you? *(After she steps in)* You look as if you'd seen a ghost.

Alice *(livid):* Did you see it?

(The driver shakes his head. She pays her fare. The bus leaves. In the park, the same branches appear to be moving slightly.)

JACQUES TOURNEUR: *CAT PEOPLE* (1942)

MARTIN SCORSESE A B-film like *Cat People* only cost $134,000, but it touched a chord in America by venturing into hitherto unexplored territory: a young bride's fear of her own sexual-

Cat People (1942): In Tourneur's films the characters are not in control of their lives. Simone Simon is consumed by malevolent feline spirits.

ity. When her deepest feelings for her husband are aroused, the heroine is overwhelmed by shame and guilt. She seems to be consumed by a malevolent spirit, or, if you will, by her inner demons.

SCENE: "MOIRA SESTRA"

Serbian-born Irena (Simone Simon) is celebrating her wedding to Oliver (Kent Smith) at a restaurant, when she is greeted by a strange feline woman (Elizabeth Russell).

Woman: Moira sestra.

(Irena is deeply affected by the words.)

Woman *(staring at her)*: Moira sestra?

Oliver *(noticing Irena's dismay)*: Now wait a minute. It can't be that serious. Just one single word.

Irena *(very pale)*: She greeted me. She called me sister!

JACQUES TOURNEUR: *CAT PEOPLE* (1942)

MARTIN SCORSESE Tourneur's films undermined a key principle of classical fiction, the notion that people are in control of themselves. Tourneur's characters were moved by forces they didn't even understand. Their curse was not fate in the Greek sense: it was not an external force; it dwelled within their own psyche. In its own unassuming way, *Cat People* was arguably as important as *Citizen Kane* in the development of a more mature American cinema.

In Tourneur's second film with producer Val Lewton, *I Walked with a Zombie*, the heroine is a nurse assigned to a catatonic woman in the West Indies; she is drawn into a parallel world when she seeks the help of sorcerers to cure her patient.

SCENE: "ONLY DEATH AND DECAY"

As she sails towards St. Sebastian with her new employer, Paul Holland (Tom Conway), Betsy (Frances Dee) is contemplating the ocean scintillating under the stars. Throughout the scene, the native crew can be heard chanting in the background.

Betsy's inner voice: It seemed only a few days before I met Mr. Holland in Antigua. We boarded the boat for St. Sebastian. It was all just as I'd imagined it. I looked at those great glowing stars. I felt the warm wind on my cheek. I breathed deep and every bit of me inside myself said, "How beautiful!"

(Her reverie is suddenly interrupted.)

Paul Holland *(off-screen)*: It's not beautiful!

Betsy *(pivoting to face him)*: You read my thoughts, Mr. Holland.

Paul Holland: It's easy enough to read the thoughts of a newcomer. Everything seems beautiful because you don't understand. Those flying fish . . . they are not leaping for joy, they are jumping in terror. Bigger fish want to eat them. That luminous water, it takes its gleam from millions of tiny dead bodies. The glitter of putrescence. There's no beauty here, only death and decay.

Betsy: You can't really believe that.

(A shooting star streaks the sky.)

Paul Holland *(off-screen)*: Everything good dies here . . . *(On-screen)* Even the stars.

JACQUES TOURNEUR: *I WALKED WITH A ZOMBIE* (1943)

MARTIN SCORSESE Jacques Tourneur was a modest craftsman; he compared his work to that of a carpenter who simply carves the chair or table that he has been hired to build. But years later, at the end of his career, Tourneur confessed that he had always been passionately interested in the supernatural. A bit of a psychic himself, he made films about the supernatural because he believed in it and had even experienced it firsthand.

How did he smuggle this contraband? Tourneur relied on the imagination of the audience. "When spectators are sitting in a darkened theater and recognize their own insecu-

I Walked with a Zombie (1943): Tom Conway points out the dangers of a hidden world to Frances Dee as they sail to the West Indies (top). The eerie mood persists on land (bottom) when a catatonic Christine Gordon is taken to the local sorcerer.

Letter from an Unknown Woman (1948): Louis Jourdan and Joan Fontaine's imaginary romance on an imaginary train. Max Ophuls's visual choreography creates a deceptively romantic mood.

rity in that of the protagonists on the screen," he remarked, "then they will accept the most unbelievable situations and follow the director wherever he wants to take them."

Tourneur's twilight zone was a labyrinth. His were perilous journeys into the unknown and sometimes into the occult. Reality remained opaque and rarely were people what they appeared to be; they stood at the frontier of a hidden world—a shimmering canvas of distant murmurs and deep shadows. There was a muted disenchantment in Tourneur's films, a strange melancholy, the eerie feeling of having embarked on an adventure from which there was no return.

After Tourneur opened Pandora's box, things were never the same. It may have gone unnoticed at first, but a strange darkness crept into American films. A feeling of insecurity, disorientation and foreboding, as though the ground could suddenly give way under your feet.

Again appearances were as deceptive as they were beautiful in Max Ophuls's elegies. The romantic decor was a trap. This was a carnival of illusions—an imaginary journey for an imaginary romance. Ophuls was an "angel in exile" in Hollywood. The Viennese maestro suffered years of unemployment until producer John Houseman gave him a chance to adapt Stefan Zweig's novella, *Letter from an Unknown Woman*. It was his valentine to Vienna and a farewell to the culture of his youth.

SCENE: **AN IMAGINARY JOURNEY**

Lisa (Joan Fontaine) and Stefan (Louis Jourdan) face each other in a mock railroad car. Behind them is a large curtained window through which painted scenery is passing inside a diorama.

Lisa *(fondling a rose)*: When my father was alive, we traveled a lot. We went nearly everywhere. We had wonderful times.

Stefan: I didn't know you traveled so much.

Lisa: Oh, yes.

Stefan: Perhaps we've been to some of the same places.

Lisa: No . . . I don't think so. We're in Venice.

Stefan: Yes, we've arrived. Now where would you like to go next? France? England? Russia?

Lisa: Switzerland.

Stefan *(rising from his seat)*: Switzerland! Excuse me one moment while I talk with the engineer.

(Stefan opens the compartment door and walks out to a booth in which an old woman is seated.)

Old woman: You and the lady, are you enjoying the trip?

Stefan: Very much. We've decided on Switzerland. *(He takes out some money and hands it to the old woman.)*

Old woman: Oh, thank you. *(Shouting to the conductor)* Switzerland!

(Cut to a tired-looking old man working the machine that moves the scenery.)

Old man: Switzerland!

(He moves a lever to change the scenery, blows a whistle, begins to pedal a bicycle and turns a wheel to start the music. Cut to Lisa and Stefan in the compartment.)

Stefan *(pulling her to him)*: Now, you know far too much about me already and I know almost nothing about you . . . except that you've traveled a great deal.

MAX OPHULS: *LETTER FROM AN UNKNOWN WOMAN* (1948)

MARTIN SCORSESE Ophuls's camera and his heroine moved in unison. The fluid visual choreography allowed you to experience Joan Fontaine's every heartbeat. For a brief moment, happiness appeared within her reach, but Stefan would always remain unattainable.

Cold reality sets in at the train station, the real one. Lisa will never travel with Stefan, the frivolous pianist on whom she has projected her passions. She's left behind, pregnant with the child conceived that magical night.

SCENE: **THE COLD REALITY**

Stefan, the frivolous pianist, is leaving Vienna to give a concert in Milan. At the station Lisa stops at the gate to look for Stefan. She sees him among the people boarding the train. A woman's voice is heard calling him. It is one of his many female admirers.

Stefan: How long have you been here? *(He takes Lisa's hand.)* I don't want to go. Do you believe that?

Lisa *(nodding)*: I'll be here when you get back . . .

Stefan *(raising her face to his)*: Say "Stefan" the way you said it last night.

Lisa: Stefan.

Stefan: It's as though you'd said it all your life.

Train conductor *(in the background)*: Better hurry, sir.

Female voice *(off-screen)*: Stefan!

Stefan *(to the woman)*: Yes, yes.

(He moves away from Lisa and runs toward the train. Her face is framed by the spikes of the fence.)

Stefan *(off-screen to Lisa)*: It won't be long. I'll be back in two weeks!

(Lisa watches the train leave, and begins to cry. She turns and walks away with her back to the camera.)

MAX OPHULS: *LETTER FROM AN UNKNOWN WOMAN* (1948)

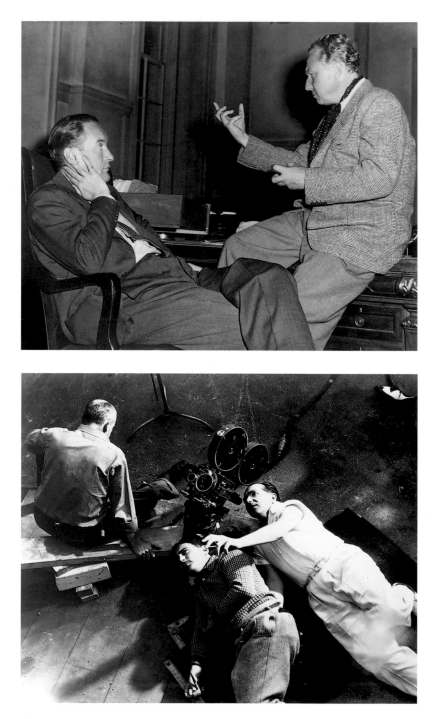

Expatriate Directors: Many of the Europeans who arrived in Hollywood in the 1940s, escaping fascism, were fascinated by crime. Douglas Sirk (top) is seen here directing George Sanders in *Lured*; Fritz Lang (bottom) behind the camera on *You and Me*.

Max Ophuls (top) with Joan Fontaine on the set of *Letter from an Unknown Woman;*
and André de Toth (bottom) rehearsing Raymond Burr in *Pitfall*.

Scarlet Street (1945): Lang shows the potential for violence in domestic life with a hen-pecked Edward G. Robinson who is tempted to kill his wife, Rosalind Ivan (above). The violence becomes real when Robinson realizes that Joan Bennett (right), the prostitute for whom he has stolen company funds, is taking him for a ride.

MARTIN SCORSESE Ophuls was just one of the European expatriates, many of them refugees from fascism, who were largely responsible for the exploration of these new, darker territories. The others were renowned directors such as Fritz Lang, Alfred Hitchcock, Otto Preminger, Billy Wilder, but also lesser-known names such as Douglas Sirk, Robert Siodmak, Edgar Ulmer, André de Toth. To them, crime was a source of fascination. It allowed them to probe the nature of evil—ordinary evil in ordinary American lives.

SCENE: **THE KITCHEN KNIFE**
An unhappily married cashier, Christopher Cross (Edward G. Robinson), is cutting liver in the kitchen when his wife Adele (Rosalind Ivan) returns home.
Christopher: Hello, Adele. I dropped over at the butcher shop like you told me to. I got a nice piece of liver.

Adele: How long have you known Katharine March? Answer me!

(Christopher stops and points the knife at his wife.)

Christopher: I don't know what you're talking about.

Adele: How long have you known her?

Christopher: Now, don't get excited, dear. (Moving toward her) Let me help you off with your coat.

Adele: You're the one that's excited. Get away from me with that knife! Do you want to cut my throat?

(He drops the kitchen knife which remains embedded in the floor.)

FRITZ LANG: SCARLET STREET (1945)

MARTIN SCORSESE Every man was a potential criminal. Monstrosity was something banal. The criminal world could not be conveniently isolated within the urban underworld as in the old gangster film. It was everywhere, lurking under the surface. A common man falling in a trap as he succumbs first to vice, then to murder. This was Fritz Lang's favorite plot—reality turning into a nightmare.

SCENE: **THE ICE PICK**

Adele's first husband is found to be still alive. Christopher is free to marry Kitty March (Joan

Bennett), the prostitute he has been keeping and for whom he has embezzled company funds. He runs to her boudoir, convinced that she will choose him over her conman lover Johnny. She is on her bed in a negligée.

Kitty: Why did you come here?

Christopher: To ask you to marry me.

Kitty: What about your wife?

Christopher: I haven't any wife. That's finished.

Kitty: For God's sake, you didn't . . .

Christopher: Her husband turned up. I'm free. *(She buries her face in a pillow.)* I don't care what's happened. I can marry you now. I want you to be my wife. We'll go away together. Way far off so you can forget this other man. Please don't cry, Kitty.

Kitty *(rising and facing him)*: I'm not crying, you fool. I'm laughing.

Christopher: Kitty!

Kitty: Oh, you idiot. How can a man be so dumb!

Christopher: Kitty!!

(Shocked, he steps back and bumps into the ice bucket. He picks up the ice pick.)

Kitty: I wanted to laugh in your face ever since I first met you. You're old and ugly and I'm sick of you. Sick, sick, sick!

Christopher: Kitty, for Heaven's sake!

Kitty *(sitting defiantly with her hands on her hips)*: You kill Johnny? I'd like to see you try. Why, he'd break every bone in your body. He's a man. You wanna marry me? You? Get out of here! Get out! Get away from me. *(As he moves menacingly toward her with the ice pick)* Chris! Chris! Get away from me! Chris! Chris!

(She tries to hide under the bed covers. He stabs her repeatedly.)

FRITZ LANG: *SCARLET STREET* (1945)

FRITZ LANG (1967) Violence has become, in my opinion, a definite point in a script. It has a dramaturgical reason to be there. I don't think people believe in the devil with the horns and the forked tail and therefore they don't believe in punishment after they are dead. So the question was for me: What do people believe? What are people fearing? That is physical pain. And physical pain comes from violence. That I think is today the only thing that people really fear. And therefore it has become a definite part of life and naturally also of scripts.

MARTIN SCORSESE The phrase "film noir" was coined by the French critics in 1946, when they discovered the Hollywood productions they had missed during the German occupation. This was not a specific genre like the Gangster Film, but rather a mood which was best described by this line from Edward G. Ulmer's *Detour*: "Which ever way you turn, fate sticks out its foot to trip you."

SCENE: **HAUNTED MEMORY**

Al Roberts (Tom Neal) recalls his nightmare when he hears the jukebox in a Las Vegas diner:

Voice-over: Did you ever wanna forget anything? Did you ever want to cut away a piece of your memory or blot it out? You can't, you know, no matter how hard you try. You can change the scenery, but sooner or later you'll get a whiff of perfume or somebody will say a certain phrase, or maybe hum something. Then you're licked again.

EDGAR G. ULMER: *DETOUR* (1946)

MARTIN SCORSESE In *Detour*, down-and-out pianist Tom Neal hitchhikes his way West to join his fiancée. His life starts unraveling when the man who has given him a lift dies unexpectedly. Doom was written on Tom Neal's face. He was bewildered, and afraid to go to the police. Keeping the dead man's car and cash was definitely a mistake. But an even bigger mistake was picking up a female hitchhiker.

Detour (1946): Several twists of fate place an ordinary man (Tom Neal) in an inextricable situation which culminates in his strangling a hitchhiker (Ann Savage).

SCENE: **THE HITCHHIKER FROM HELL**

At a gas station, Al Roberts (Tom Neal) picks up Vera (Ann Savage). She looks asleep, but suddenly speaks.
Vera: Where did you leave his body? Where did you leave the owner of this car? You're not fooling anyone. This buggy belongs to a guy named Haskell. That's not you, mister. It just so happens I rode with Charlie Haskell. All the way from Shreveport.

EDGAR G. ULMER: *DETOUR* (1946)

MARTIN SCORSESE *Detour* was shot in six days for only $20,000. Ulmer could only rely on his resourcefulness. In fact, his idiosyncratic style grew out of such drastic limitations. This is why he has become such an inspiration over the years to low-budget filmmakers.

When a second, outrageous twist of fate crushed Tom Neal, leaving him a murderer, Ulmer couldn't even afford any special effects. He simply let the shot go in and out of focus repeatedly—an appropriate reflection of the character's disoriented mental state.

SCENE: **A SECOND TWIST OF FATE**

A Los Angeles motel. Al has inadvertently killed Vera, strangling her when he pulled on the telephone cord which she had twisted around her neck. As Al approaches the body lying on the bed, the camera pans around the room. Various objects are revealed, in and out of focus: her face, the telephone, her perfume bottles, a bottle of whiskey, her shoes, an opened gift parcel.

Al's voice-over: The world is full of sceptics. I know. I am one myself. And the Haskell business: How many of you would belive he fell out of the car? Now after killing Vera without really meaning to do it, how many of you would believe it wasn't premeditated? Vera was dead. And I was her murderer. Murderer!

EDGAR G. ULMER: *DETOUR* (1946)

MARTIN SCORSESE The hitchhiker's journey turned into an ironic morality play. Film noir showed how quickly an ordinary man could lose it all when he strayed from his path. Lured by the prospect of sinful pleasures, he ended up suffering hellish retribution.

BILLY WILDER Film noir! You know, when I made a picture, I never classified it or said , "This is a comedy." I waited until the preview and if they laughed a lot, I said it was a comedy . . . or a serious picture . . . or film noir . . . I never heard that expression in those days. I just made pictures that I would have liked to see. And if I was lucky, it coincided with the taste of the audience.

MARTIN SCORSESE Film noir revealed the dark underbelly of American urban life. Its denizens were private eyes, rogue cops, white-collar criminals, femmes fatales. As Raymond Chandler put it: "The streets were dark with something more than night." *After Double Indemnity*, you couldn't take anything for granted anymore. Not even suburbia. Not even the supermarkets of Southern California.

SCENE: **THE BLACK WIDOW**

Phyllis Dietrichson (Barbara Stanwyck) and Walter Neff (Fred MacMurray) meet at a supermarket after their crime, the murder of her husband. They stand in adjacent aisles, separated by shelves of canned goods.

Phyllis *(wearing dark sunglasses)*: I loved you, Walter, and I hated him. But I wasn't going to do anything about it, not until I met you. You planned the whole thing. I only wanted him dead.

Walter: And I'm the one who fixed it so he was dead. Is that what you're telling me?

Phyllis *(removing her sunglasses)*: And nobody is pulling out. We went into this together and we're coming out at the end together, straight down the line for both of us. Remember?

(She turns around and leaves him bewildered.)

BILLY WILDER: *DOUBLE INDEMNITY* (1944)

ANDRÉ DE TOTH Life is a betrayal and, you know, sometimes you betray yourself too. Let's have the guts to admit it. There isn't anybody born here lately who didn't play dirty sometime, somewhere, in his life. So why hide it? Truth, honesty, that's my key in filmmaking. In life, too, I try.

MARTIN SCORSESE André de Toth was one of the most persistent of the expatriate smugglers. In *Crime Wave* he undermined the old cliché that in America you can always get another break, a second chance. Gene Nelson plays an ex-convict trying to go straight, who is haunted by his past. Even a sympathetic parole officer can't save

Double Indemnity (1944): After Wilder's movie, even suburbia wasn't safe. Crime lurks everywhere: in the aisle of a local supermarket, Barbara Stanwyck and Fred MacMurray confer after the murder of her husband.

Nelson from Sterling Hayden, the relentless cop who presumes that he is guilty.

SCENE: OUT OF THE PAST

Awakened in the middle of the night, Steve Lacey (Gene Nelson) sits in bed and picks up the telephone.
Caller *(off-screen)*: Is this Steve Lacey?
Steve Lacey: Allo? This is Lacey.
(The caller has hung up. He is a mobster who has just

killed a policeman and is trying to implicate Lacey.)
Lacey *(to his wife Ellen played by Phyllis Kirk)*: They are always passing through town. Trying to put the bite on me for this or that. But I told you how it would be.
Ellen: I didn't mind, did I? I loved you and now that I've got ya, I care a lot less.
Lacey: I can't figure what you see in a guy like me.
Ellen *(snuggling against him)*: I see a guy who's swell.
(Later at the police station, Detective Sgt. Sims,

Crime Wave (1954): Phyllis Kirk watches as her husband, Gene Nelson, is arrested by Sterling Hayden, a relentless cop who won't forgive Nelson's criminal past. There are no second chances for de Toth's protagonist.

played by Sterling Hayden, discusses the criminal case with his inspectors.)

Inspector: Lacey's gone pretty straight since he got out of jail.

Sims: Yeah, I know. Sober. Industrious. Expert mechanic on airplane engines. A pilot before they sent him up. Now works at a private airport in Sunland.

Inspector: Right.

Sims: Call him!

(The phone rings in the Laceys' bedroom. In a close shot on the telephone, we see Lacey's arm reaching to pick it up. Ellen's hand stops him.)

Ellen *(off-screen):* Don't answer it, Steve. Let it ring. They just want what they all want. Let them think that you're away and that you're not here and they'll leave you alone.

Lacey *(off-screen):* Once you've done a bit, nobody leaves you alone. Somebody's always on your back.

Ellen *(off-screen):* Steve . . .

(Cut back to the police station: Sims's suspicions are now confirmed.)

Sims: No answer.

(He hangs up. Back at the apartment: the phone is not ringing anymore.)

Ellen *(off-screen):* There you see! I told you!

(Cut to the police station.)

Sims: Don't look so good for Mr. Lacey.

ANDRÉ DE TOTH: *CRIME WAVE* (1954)

ANDRÉ DE TOTH How long has one to pay for a mistake, for a misstep in one's life? When is enough enough? There is no reprieve in film noir. You just keep paying for your sins.

SCENE: "ONCE A CROOK, ALWAYS A CROOK."

Sims arrests Lacey in spite of the latter's parole officer. He has a toothpick in his mouth.

Sims *(to parole officer):* You stay on your side of the fence. I'm looking for a cop killer.

Parole officer: I'm on my side. I don't take things for granted. I check and recheck. Lacey's made good with me. I have faith in him.

Sims: Once a crook, always a crook.

Parole officer: That's nonsense and you know it. Sick men get well again.

Sims: Yeah? You hate to lose a patient. Well, you gonna lose this one. *(He turns to the cops.)* Mark, you stay here with a couple of men and find that dough. Don't worry about wrecking the joint, just find it.

Cop: Right.

Sims: All right, hotshot. Put out your hands. *(He handcuffs Lacey, then notices the wife's reaction.)* You don't like that, do you, Mrs. Lacey? Well, just remember it could happen to you if you're covering up for this guy. So don't try to walk out on us. You are a material witness.

Lacey *(to his wife):* Don't stay here, Ellen, forget about me. Get out of town.

(She tries to get up from the armchair, but Sims pushes her back.)

Sims: Are you finished, Mr. Lacey?

(With his thumb Sims points him towards the exit.)

ANDRÉ DE TOTH: *CRIME WAVE* (1954)

MARTIN SCORSESE Ida Lupino often used film noir visuals but for her own, very specific purposes. In her films, it was young women who went through hell when their middle-class security was shattered by a traumatic experience: bigamy, parental abuse, unwanted pregnancy, and rape. Lupino the director would force the audience to experience from the inside and share the ordeal of her heroines.

In an unusual move, actress Ida Lupino had become a director in 1949 after being suspended by Warner Bros. She seized the opportunity to form a production company with her husband Collier Young. They developed their own projects, making a policy of discovering young talent and tackling unglamorous subjects, such as the rape in *Outrage* (page 114).

The film presents the ultimate female nightmare not as a melodrama, but as a subdued behavioral study that captures the banality of evil in an ordinary small town. Beyond the horror of the crime, Lupino illuminates the changes in the victim's psyche. The wounded young woman cannot handle a relationship anymore, let alone the marriage she has planned. She will spend the rest of the film learning how to overcome her pain and despair.

In Joseph H. Lewis's *Gun Crazy*, the focus was not on the victim, but on the criminals themselves. You were compelled to share their fear and even their exhilaration. The audience was pulled into the action and became an accomplice. Of course, the fascinating pair of *Gun Crazy* (page 116) belonged to the outlaw tradition of the thirties—the tradition that would culminate in the sixties with Arthur Penn's *Bonnie and Clyde*. But in Lewis's landmark film, the renegades were wild animals! Sex and violence were totally intertwined.

Outrage (1950): Ida Lupino depicts rape, not as a melodrama but as a subdued behavioral study of the victim (Mala Powers) and of evil in an ordinary small town.

Gun Crazy (1950): Lewis focused on the criminals, a wild pair in the outlaw tradition of the thirties (played by John Dall and Peggy Cummins), intertwining sex and violence.

SCENE: "WE GO TOGETHER LIKE GUN AND AMMUNITION."

Laurie (Peggy Cummins) lures Bart (John Dall) into a spiral of crime and passion. They are driving away after a holdup.

Bart *(driving)*: You can't shoot a man just because he hesitates.

Laurie *(in glasses and a black beret)*: Maybe not, but you can sure scare them off, like that hotel clerk.

Bart: No, Laurie, I, I . . .

Laurie: You know something . . .

Bart: What?

Laurie *(putting her arm under his)*: I love you. I love you more than anything else in the world . . .

(Later, after another bank holdup, Bart stops her from gunning down a manager in the street. They make their getaway with a police car in hot pursuit.)

Bart *(looking back at the police car, holding a gun)*: You were gonna kill that man.

Laurie *(driving)*: He'd have killed us if he had the chance.

(Bart moves to the back seat as the police car comes closer and closer. He aims his gun, but can't shoot.)

Laurie: Shoot, why don't you shoot? Shoot! Shoot, do you hear me?

Bart *(taking aim again)*: All right.

(He fires at a front tire. The police car careens off the road into a tree.)

Laurie: Get 'em?

Bart *(moving back into his seat, next to her)*: Yeah.

(Laurie's face lights up; she represses a smile.)

JOSEPH H. LEWIS: *GUN CRAZY* (1950)

MARTIN SCORSESE First and foremost, film noir was a style. It combined realism and expressionism, the use of real locations and elaborate shadowplays.

Here the ace cinematographer John Alton deserves a mention. The Hungarian-born master

"painted with light" (this was the title of his 1949 textbook, which we were still using as students in the sixties): extreme black and white contrasts, isolated sources of lighting, ominous camera placement, deep perspective . . . The most striking examples of Alton's work are found in Anthony Mann's early films, such as *T-Men* (page 118) and *Raw Deal.*

These were small B-productions where Alton was free to experiment and often took unusual risks. His chiaroscuros alone conjured up the noir mood. "There is no doubt in my mind that the prettiest music is sad," he remarked. "And the most beautiful photography is in a low key, with rich blacks."

SCENE: "TOP-DRAWER CROOK."

Dennis O'Brien (Dennis O'Keefe), an undercover agent investigating a counterfeiting ring, cannot betray his emotions when gangster Moxie (Charles McGraw) decides to execute O'Brien's friend and partner Tony Genaro (Alfred Ryder) who has been caught redhanded.

Moxie *(to Tony)*: Busy little man, eh, snooper?

(Behind him, in the background, we see O'Brien and the rest of the gang entering the dark room.)

Tony *(sweating)*: Almost had you. All of you.

O'Brien *(in close-up)*: Tony . . .

Tony *(in close-up)*: And you, Dennis. So smart. Top-drawer crook. Lived with me and never caught on. *(O'Brien's face registers as he takes the hint about the top drawer.)* Top-drawer crook. Always so sharp, always knew all the angles.

(Moxie guns Tony down off-screen. The shot is heard over O'Brien's face.)

Tony *(whispering off-screen before collapsing)*: Sucker.

(As O'Brien lowers his head, the brim of his hat shades his eyes.)

ANTHONY MANN: *T-MEN* (1948)

117

T-Men (1948): Cinematographer John Alton, more than anyone, created the look of the film noir by "painting with light." Here Dennis O'Keefe is grilling Wallace Ford about the counterfeiters.

MARTIN SCORSESE The paranoia of film noir reached its high point in Robert Aldrich's *Kiss Me Deadly*. Out of the dark, a haunted woman appears to private eye Mike Hammer. She is running away from a mental institution and an unbearable secret. She is not mad though, merely innocent. Destined to be a sacrificial lamb.

SCENE: **RESURRECTION**

Mike Hammer (Ralph Meeker) lies unconscious, while Christina (Cloris Leachman) is being tortured. Only her naked legs are visible. When her screams stop, Dr.

Soberin's (Albert Dekker) voice is heard off-screen:

Dr. Soberin's voice: She passed out.

Gangster's voice: I'll bring her to.

Dr. Soberin's voice: If you revive her, do you know what that would be? Resurrection, that's what it would be. And do you know what resurrection means? It means raise the dead. And just who do you think you are that you think you can raise the dead?

(Hammer regains consciousness. From the floor, all he sees are Christina's naked legs and the pair of pliers held by one of the gangsters.)

ROBERT ALDRICH: *KISS ME DEADLY* (1955)

Kiss Me Deadly (1955): Gaby Rodgers opening Pandora's (radioactive) box at the end of Aldrich's movie, the apogee of film noir paranoia.

MARTIN SCORSESE Stylized lighting and composition conveyed a deranged world. There was no moral compass anymore. Aldrich even turned Mickey Spillane's detective Mike Hammer into an ambiguous figure, a guy who's treated like dirt by everybody and described as "a sleazy, despicable bedroom dick." Aldrich's point, an important one during those McCarthy times, was: "The end never justifies the means."

At the end of *Kiss Me Deadly*, the duplicitous woman who stole the radioactive package from a secret government project (page 119) was like the wife of Lot who refused to heed the warnings. Aldrich's tale led to a few cryptic, threatening words: "Manhattan Project . . . Los Alamos . . . Trinity . . . " This time, opening Pandora's box meant universal annihilation—the Apocalypse.

I am often asked by younger filmmakers: Why do I need to look at old movies? The only response I can give them is: I still consider myself a student. Yes, I have made a number of pictures in the past twenty years. But the more pictures I make, the more I realize that I really don't know. I'm always looking for something or someone that I can learn from. This is what I tell young filmmakers and film students: Do what painters used to do, and probably still do. Study the old masters. Enrich your palette. Expand the canvas. There's always so much more to learn.

Take a forgotten B-film like *Silver Lode*. It was directed by Allan Dwan, one of the unheralded pioneers who had made the first of his four hundred films back in 1911. At the end of his long career, he was relegated to low-budget genre films. But you have to admire the beauty of the sweeping tracking shots literally guiding a desperate John Payne toward his final sanctuary, the town church. Dwan's finest movies featured simple people, pastoral landscapes and the rural America

of a bygone era. Yet behind the lyrical images of the old West, *Silver Lode* suggests the fragility of our democratic institutions. On the day of his wedding, John Payne should be the happiest man in Silver Lode. Instead, he has to fight for his life when he is unjustly accused of a murder and ostracized by the community. Daringly, the fugitive's bride-to-be convinces the town that he is not guilty by forging a federal warrant. A church bell and a fantastic fraud save the day. Persecuted for the wrong reasons, Payne is pardoned for the wrong reasons. This was the era of the blacklists; political messages had to be smuggled in— cloaked in metaphors. Actually, the name of the villain played by Dan Duryea was McCarty.

SCENE: **A WITCH-HUNT ON THE 4TH OF JULY**
McCarty (Dan Duryea) is dead. Dan Ballard (John Payne) has been cleared by a fake telegram concocted by his fiancée Rose (Lizabeth Scott). He has survived his ordeal and now faces the mayor and the villagers who hunted him. They all look embarrassed or ashamed.
Mayor: Dan, there isn't much that I can say, but I think I can speak for all of us . . . We're sorry.
Dan: You're sorry! A moment ago, you wanted to kill me. And you forced me to kill. To defend myself, to save my own life. You wouldn't believe what I said. A man's life can hang in the balance. On a piece of paper. And you're sorry!
ALLAN DWAN: *SILVER LODE* (1954)

MARTIN SCORSESE The fifties. This is a fascinating era when the subtext became as important—or sometimes more important—than the apparent subject matter. Take Douglas Sirk's *All That Heaven Allows* or Nicholas Ray's *Bigger Than Life*, both made in the mid-fifties. These were not B-movies; these were big scale pictures with major studio stars. Both Sirk and Ray stayed

Silver Lode (1954): Dwan's sweeping shots literally guide a desperate John Payne, falsely accused of murder, to refuge in the town church.

within the rules: their films had the required happy ending. Yet they hinted at the dangers inherent in conforming to society's conventions.

SCENE: FAR FROM WALDEN POND

Carey (Jane Wyman) is a widow, Ron Kirby (Rock Hudson) a gardener. His retreat is a bucolic mill nestled in a snow-covered New England landscape. In the living room Carey looks at the pond through a large bay-window covered with frost.

Carey: What a beautiful view of the pond. Why, you can see for miles.

Ron: The sun comes up right over that hill. Do you like it?

Carey: Why, it's unbelievable.

Ron: Let's take your boots off . . .

A small-town country club, Ron is introduced by Carey's best friend Sarah, played by Agnes Moorehead, to the social elite.

Sarah *(to a matron):* Mr. Kirby.

Ron: How do you do?

Mrs. Humphrey: What's this I hear about your . . . oh, haven't I seen you somewhere before?

Ron: Well, Mrs. Humphrey, probably in your garden. I've been pruning your trees for the last three years.

All That Heaven Allows (1955): In Sirk's indictment of American small-town life, Jane Wyman plays a lonely widow in love with her gardener (Rock Hudson).

Mrs. Humphrey: Yes, of course. Sarah, I really must be going. *(Mrs. Humphrey leaves the group.)*
Sarah *(following her)*: Excuse me, I'll be right back.
Later, the couple is back at Ron's mill.
Ron: Are you saying you don't want to marry me?
Carey: Oh no, I'm not saying that. I'm just asking you to be patient. It's only a question of time.
Ron: Only of time.
Carey: Well, right now, everybody's talking about us. We're a local sensation. And like Sarah said, if the people get used to seeing us together, then, then maybe they'll accept us.
Ron: You mean, we'll be invited to all the cocktail parties. And of course, Sarah will see to it that I get into the country club.
Carey: I can see that you don't want to listen to anybody's ideas but your own, and you're trying to make me choose between you and the children.
Ron: No, Carey, you're the one that made it a question of choosing. So you're the one that'll have to choose.
Carey: Alright. It's all over.
(She leaves. He is too stunned to try and stop her.)
DOUGLAS SIRK: *ALL THAT HEAVEN ALLOWS* (1955)

MARTIN SCORSESE Furthermore, these were "Americanas," the most wholesome genre of the period. Jane Wyman, the widow in Sirk's *All That Heaven Allows*, is not rejected by her community; she is immersed in it. Her world becomes unhinged when she falls in love with Rock Hudson, a much younger man who happens to be her gardener. A spiritual descendant of Thoreau, he represents a solid and serene individualism that seems sadly out of place in the New England of the fifties.

Once she surrenders to her milieu's pressures, Jane Wyman is trapped. She is left suffocating in their world of pretense and illusions, far from Hudson's Walden Pond. Home, family, social roles can't fulfill the pursuit of happiness anymore; somehow they have become the instruments of repression. Beneath the surface of the seemingly ideal setting, lies a sharp indictment of American small-town life. If you can't have a life, settle for its imitation—a TV set. This is what Jane Wyman receives from her children as a substitute for her lost love. Television, the movies' rival medium in the fifties, was cast as the ultimate symbol of alienation.

DOUGLAS SIRK (1970s) Anything indirect is stronger, in many cases at least, because you leave it or hand it over to the imagination of your audience. I have always been trusting my audience to have imagination. Otherwise they should stay out of the cinema. You have to leave something open. The moment you start preaching in a film, the moment you want to teach your audience, you're making a bad film.

SCENE: "LIFE'S PARADE AT YOUR FINGERTIPS."

Carey Scott (Jane Wyman) has yielded to the pressures of her friends and above all her two children (William Reynolds, Gloria Talbot). She has terminated her relationship with Ron. At Christmas, she is rewarded by her children. The doorbell rings.

Ned (*the son*): There's your present now.

(*A dejected Carey looks up.*)

Ned: Mother, Merry Christmas.

(*A TV set is brought in.*)

Delivery Man: Merry Christmas, Mrs. Scott.

(*Carey is speechless as they set up the television.*)

Delivery Man: And it's easy to operate. All you have to do is turn that dial and you have all the company you want. Right there on the screen.

(*The camera dollies in toward her black and white reflection on the TV screen.*)

Delivery Man (*off-screen*): Drama, comedy, life's parade at your fingertips.

DOUGLAS SIRK: *ALL THAT HEAVEN ALLOWS* (1955)

MARTIN SCORSESE Like Douglas Sirk, Nicholas Ray offered both the American family in suburbia and the psychotic undercurrents, the conventions and the contradictions, the sugar and the poison. In *Bigger Than Life*, James Mason (page 124) portrays a frustrated schoolteacher who undergoes personality changes when he becomes hooked on cortisone, then an experimental drug. Sometimes he feels that he is ten feet tall! The cortisone acts as a catalyst; it reveals a mental and spiritual dissatisfaction; it fuels Mason's growing desire to escape the dull existence that stifles his soul. Mason's family goes through hell as he starts questioning every tenet of family life in the fifties: momism, Sunday school, little league sports, and even the egalitarian principles of American education.

SCENE: THE SUGAR AND THE POISON

Ed (James Mason), his wife Lou (Barbara Rush) and their son Richie (Christopher Olsen) are eating in the dining room.

Ed: Lou, it will be better for all of us if you clearly understand one thing. I will not tolerate your attempts to undermine my program for Richard.

Lou: Yes, darling.

Ed: Will you have enough regard not to speak in that hypocritical tone of voice? I see through you as clearly as I see through this glass pitcher. If you imagine I'm going to be fooled by all this sweetness and meekness, "Yes, darling, no, darling," you're even a bigger idiot than I took you for! It clearly is over once and for all. I'm staying in this house solely for the boy's sake! As for you personally, I'm completely finished with you! There's nothing left. Our marriage is over. In my mind I've divorced you. You're not my wife any longer, I'm not your husband any longer!

NICHOLAS RAY: *BIGGER THAN LIFE* (1956)

NICHOLAS RAY (1974) My heroes are no more neurotic than the audience. Unless you can feel that a hero is just as fucked up as you are and that you would make the same mistakes that he would make, you can have no satisfaction when he does commit a heroic act, because then you can say: "Hell, I could have done that too!" And that's the obligation of the filmmaker—to give a heightened sense of experience to the people who pay to come and see his work.

Bigger Than Life (1956): Ray probes
every aspect of American morality when
James Mason (with Christopher Olsen and
Barbara Rush) goes mad under the influence
of cortisone (then an experimental drug).

Ed reads from the Bible the story of Abraham slaying his son. He is holding a knife as his wife listens.

Ed: "And they came to the place of which God had told him. And Abraham built an altar there and laid the wood in order and bound Isaac his son and laid him on the altar upon the wood. And Abraham stretched forth his hand and took the knife to slay his son."

Lou: But, Ed, you didn't read it all. God stopped Abraham.

Ed: God was wrong!

(He pushes her and locks her inside a closet . . .)

Lou: No, Ed! No, Ed, no! Richie, climb out of the window! Richie! Richie! (She pounds on the door.)*

(Ed turns on the TV in the living room and rushes upstairs to his son's room. On the threshold, he raises the knife as if to strike the child. From his bed Ritchie calmly hands him a football. Suddenly, the screen turns blood red: Ed is paralyzed by a stroke.)

NICHOLAS RAY: *BIGGER THAN LIFE* (1956)

MARTIN SCORSESE Samuel Fuller's characters were no intellectuals. His was a visceral cinema—excessive, explosive. He once defined film as a battlefield: "Love, hate, action, death—in one word, emotion!" Impact was his main concern. Whether he was dealing with the Old West or Cold War America, his images were bursting with violence and sexual energy.

In *Pickup on South Street*, Richard Widmark is a pickpocket and Jean Peters a prostitute. Working on her purse in the subway, he inadvertently takes a microfilm which Communist agents are trying to smuggle out of the country.

SCENE: "I'LL DO BUSINESS WITH A RED."

Candy (Jean Peters) negotiates with Skip McCoy (Richard Widmark), the pickpocket who stole a microfilm from her purse in the subway. He is holding her tight in his arms. They could be making love.

Skip: How much is it worth to you?

Candy: What are you pushing me for?

Skip: You came here to buy, didn't you?

Skip: How much did you bring?

Candy: I don't want to talk about it.

Skip: How much?

Candy: Five hundred . . .

(He stops kissing her and brutally pushes her away. She falls on her back.)

Skip: You tell that Commie, I want a big score for that film and I want it in cash! Tonight!

Candy: What are you talking about?

Skip: You tell me, you people are supposed to have all the answers. (He rummages through her purse.)*

Candy: Tell you what? I don't . . .

Skip: C'mon, drop the act! So, you're a Red . . . Who cares, your money is as good as anybody else's! (He lifts her up.) Now get your stern up those stairs and tell your old lady what I want. I'll do business with a Red, but I don't have to believe one.

(She slaps him in the face. Hard.)

SAMUEL FULLER: *PICKUP ON SOUTH STREET* (1953)

MARTIN SCORSESE America's fate is in the hands of two outcasts. She's just a runner who doesn't even know what side she's on, while he's a cynic willing to do business with all sides. Playing both ends against the middle, Widmark defied all "isms," even patriotism. Fuller's heroes were hard to distinguish from his villains.

A former crime reporter, writer-director-producer Fuller was the most outspoken of the fifties' smugglers. He cultivated the shocks and hyperbole of the tabloid headlines. Nothing escaped his scathing irony. His work was an antidote to complacency during the Cold War. American hypocrisy was his constant target.

Pickup on South Street (1953): Fuller pits two outcasts against the system, when pickpocket Richard Widmark robs prostitute Jean Peters, inadvertently taking a Soviet microfilm from her.

The FBI agents are grilling Skip (Richard Widmark).

FBI agent: If you refuse to cooperate, you'll be as guilty as the traitors that gave Stalin the A-bomb.

Skip: Are you waving the flag at me?

FBI agent: I know something on our side you should give . . .

Skip: Get this. I didn't grift that film, and you can't prove I did.

FBI agent: Do you know what treason means?

Skip: Who cares?

FBI agent: Answer the man.

Skip: Is there a law now I gotta listen to lectures?

SAMUEL FULLER: *PICKUP ON SOUTH STREET* (1953)

SAMUEL FULLER (1989) When he said, "Don't wave the goddam flag at me," Edgar Hoover objected to that in my presence at Romanoff's table with Zanuck. He objected that an American would say, during the heat of the Cold War with Russia, "Don't wave the goddam flag at me." And Zanuck said to me, "He's right, we'll leave out goddam." Hoover got very angry: "You know damn well that's not what I mean." And Zanuck explained very simply. He was a friend of his, he knew him. "This is his character talking and that character doesn't give a goddamn about the flag. It means nothing to him. Any flag! You must be that character. Otherwise we're making a propaganda film and we don't make those kinds of propaganda films."

MARTIN SCORSESE Fuller had found a niche in B-films and genre pictures, but when the studio system collapsed, he was relegated to making low-budget independent productions. He had no money, no stars and minimal sets, but out of these limitations emerged an outstanding film, *Shock Corridor.*

A journalist pretends to be a madman in order to investigate a crime that took place in a mental hospital. Instead of winning the Pulitzer Prize, he goes mad. *Shock Corridor* was full of front page material. The inmates were the product of Cold War paranoia and Southern racism. Every form of American insanity was represented. The metaphor was crystal clear: in Fuller's vision, America had become an insane asylum.

SCENE: **AMERICA AS AN INSANE ASYLUM**

Trent, a black inmate (Hari Rhodes), carries a poster that reads: "Integration and Democracy Don't Mix. Go Home Nigger." He was institutionalized because he couldn't bear being the only black student in a Southern university. Later, Trent is sitting on a bench next to undercover journalist Johnny Barrett (Peter Breck) and shows him a pillowcase with two holes.

Trent: This baptizes a new organization. The Ku Klux.

Johnny: Sounds good.

Trent: No. Ku Klux Klan. Sounds more mysterious, more menacing, more alliterative. Ku Klux Klan. Say it.

Johnny: Ku Klux Klan.

Trent *(staccato):* K-K-K.

Johnny *(same):* K-K-K.

Trent: It'll catch on quick. *(Shaking his fist)* It'll drive those carpetbaggers back north. Scare the hell out of 'em, tar and feather 'em, hang 'em, burn 'em. *(He dons the hood . . .)*

(Trent stands on the bench, surrounded by a group of inmates, including Johnny who is visibly worried that the situation is getting out of control.)

Trent: Listen to me, Americans. America for America!

Inmate: America for Americans!

Trent *(donning the hood):* Keep our schools white!

Inmate: Keep 'em white! That's right. Keep 'em white!

Trent: I'm against Catholics!

Inmate: Hallelujah, man! Hallelujah!

Trent: Against Jews!

The Most Outspoken Smuggler: A former newspaper reporter, Samuel Fuller thrived on shocking audiences and attacking American hypocrisy.

Shock Corridor (1963): When a journalist commits himself to a mental hospital to investigate a crime, he finds every form of modern madness. A black man joins the KKK (left). In Fuller 's vision America had become an insane asylum (above).

Inmate: Hallelujah! Hallelujah! Hallelujah!

Trent: Against niggers!

Inmate: Hallelujah! Hallelujah!

Trent: Against niggers!

Inmate: Hallelujah!

Trent: Against niggers!

Inmate: Hallelujah!

Trent: *(points to another black man drinking at the water fountain):* That one! Let's get that black one before he marries my daughter!

Inmate: Hallelujah! Hallelujah!

(Led by Trent, the yelling horde of inmates rush down the corridor to grab the black man.)

SAMUEL FULLER: *SHOCK CORRIDOR* (1963)

MARTIN SCORSESE Sadly, Fuller's later career was typical of the times. To finance his unorthodox projects, he had to move to Europe. For a whole generation of smugglers, this was the end of the line.

The pioneers and the showmen were gone; the moguls were replaced by agents and executives; actors and directors were starting their own companies. Runaway production was the name of the game. To make films, you had to go to London, Paris, Madrid, or Rome. A film like Vincente Minnelli's *Two Weeks in Another Town* captured the desperation of the times. Welcome to Hollywood on the Tiber!

SCENE: **THE END OF THE GOLDEN AGE.**
An American director working in Cinecittà with a foreign crew and a second-rate cast, Maurice Krueger (Edward G. Robinson), confronts his Italian producer (Mino Doro).

Producer: You are behind schedule.

Krueger: I need two weeks to finish shooting this picture. You give me two extra weeks and I'll give you a Maurice Krueger picture. Don't you want the best

movie you can get?

Producer: No.

Krueger: Don't you have any pride in what pictures you put your name on?

Producer: No . . .

Cast and crew are watching a black and white scene from The Bad and the Beautiful *in a screening room: Kirk Douglas is confronting Lana Turner about her neurotic fixation on her father. Seated in the theater are Maurice Krueger, his star Jack Andrus (Kirk Douglas) and the Italian producer, who is flanked by two Italian actresses.*

Lana Turner *(on screen):* Turn it off, I want to get some sleep.

Krueger *(sitting on the first row):* Coccino, you international peddler. Take a good look at a movie that was made because we just couldn't sleep until we made it.

Kirk Douglas *(on screen, drawing a mustache on the father's portrait):* Laugh the way he would've laughed. That's not a god talking, that's only a man.

(The two Italian women have their hands on the producer's pants.)

Jack *(sitting behind Krueger):* Krueger, you're great.

Krueger *(reflects on this statement for a second or two):* I was great.

VINCENTE MINNELLI: *TWO WEEKS IN ANOTHER TOWN* (1962)

MARTIN SCORSESE Ironically, *Two Weeks in Another Town* was the sequel to *The Bad and the Beautiful*. Both films were directed by Minnelli, produced by John Houseman and starred Kirk Douglas. But in ten years, from 1952 to 1962, the industry had undergone tremendous changes and *Two Weeks in Another Town* was a startling mirror of Hollywood's decline.

The golden age was over and for many a veteran director this was a painful period of anguish and self-doubt.

Two Weeks in Another Town (1962): Made in Europe, Minnelli's film dramatized the decline of Hollywood. Director Edward G. Robinson has collapsed at the end of his career.

SCENE: "AM I JUST PLAIN AFRAID?"

After an argument with her husband, Clara (Claire Trevor) locks herself in the bathroom. In forcing the door open Krueger breaks the mirror hanging behind it.
Krueger: Clara, don't swallow all those sleeping pills. The doctor will just have to come up and pump out your stomach. You know how sick that makes me.
(Later that night, Krueger and Clara are lying in bed, but cannot sleep.)
Krueger: Clara? Clara? I, I look at this film I'm shooting. I like it. *(He pauses.)* What if I'm wrong? It's another calamity. Where do I go from here? Took

me two years to get this job and that was a fluke. How can a man go wrong and not know why? What's happened to me? *(She sits up and lights a cigarette.)* Is it ego? Self-indulgence? *(He sits up too.)* Or am I just plain afraid?
Clara *(cradling him like a child)*: Oh, my poor . . . I've seen the film you're shooting and it's beautiful.
VINCENTE MINNELLI: *TWO WEEKS IN ANOTHER TOWN* (1962)

5

THE DIRECTOR

AS ICONOCLAST

Frank Sinatra in Otto Preminger's *The Man with the Golden Arm.*

MARTIN SCORSESE Whereas the smuggler works undercover, and his subversion is not detected immediately, the iconoclast attacks conventions head on and his defiance sends shock waves through the industry. In Hollywood, the iconoclasts comprise the visionaries, the groundbreakers, the renegades who openly defied the system and expanded the art form. Often they were defeated; sometimes they actually made the system work for them. Hollywood has always had a love-hate relationship with those who break its rules, extolling them one moment, burning them the next.

The film industry often confused entertainment with escapism. Borrowing from real life was deemed either boring or subversive—particularly if it meant plumbing the lower depths. But back in the silent era, a few filmmakers challenged the ideals of glamor and wholesomeness by injecting a dose of reality in their films, generally within the framework of the melodrama.

D. W. Griffith, for instance, is often identified with quaint romanticism and Victorian sensibility. But more than once he soared beyond the accepted melodrama of his time. In *Broken Blossoms*, he showed how a sordid reality can destroy the purest dreams. This was the most delicate interracial romance.

Physical and spiritual suffering is what unites Lillian Gish, the waif battered by her boxing father, and Richard Barthelmess, the young Buddhist who has lost his religious fervor in the slums of London. Their bodies, like their souls, are bent or stunted. Both are broken blossoms. Only when they find each other, do they come alive. For a brief moment, they are allowed to dream before our eyes. But when the racist father discovers the situation, bigotry is exposed in its rawest form. Sweetness and compassion turn to fury and savagery. The young Chinese, who doesn't believe in violence, picks up a gun to save his beloved. He'll come too late. Her punishment is death.

Erich von Stroheim was the most outrageous of the iconoclasts. And he fell the hardest. *The Wedding March* (page 140) was a fairy tale, but a tragic one, with Fay Wray, a poor musician's daughter, in the role of Cinderella and Stroheim, the scion of an aristocratic family, as her Prince Charming. The setting was Vienna in the last days of the Hapsburg dynasty, a decadent world that both fascinated and repelled Stroheim. The city of waltzes and operettas was a pigsty. Behind the romantic exterior Stroheim revealed an ugly, cruel society ruled by greed. Rather than indulge in the splendors of imperial Vienna, he chose to expose its moral squalor. You saw the young Prince's father, a ruined aristocrat, strike a deal with a rich merchant desperate to marry off his crippled daughter. The apple blossoms offered a brief refuge, but they were an illusion. Stroheim's heroines were no madonnas. Like their male counterparts, they were always endowed with strong sexual desires. What Stroheim was after was a more honest depiction of human relationships. His images could be brutal and they inevitably got him into trouble with the censors, but at heart he was a romantic who was haunted by the loss and the corruption of love. Both lovers in *The Wedding March* (page 141) were victims: the young girl who surrendered her soul and the Prince who had not yet been corrupted by the hypocrisy of his milieu. Innocence was doomed from the start.

Stroheim paid a high price for his transgressions and his perceived intransigence. The very qualities that made him a great artist undid him. He was dubbed a megalomaniac and ended up losing control over most of his projects. They

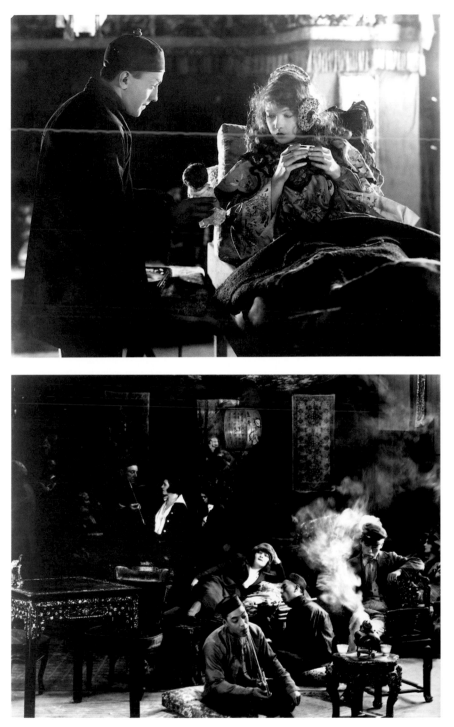

Broken Blossoms (1919): In Griffith's film two broken souls, Lillian Gish and Richard Barthelmess, find temporary solace with each other.

Broken Blossoms (1919): Richard Barthelmess plays a young Chinese man who has lost his Buddhist faith in the slums of London.

The Wedding March (1927): Von Stroheim set his movie in the decadent last years of the Hapsburg empire (above). A ruined aristocrat arranges the marriage of the crippled daughter of a rich merchant to his son (von Stroheim), who loves Fay Wray (right).

would all be eventually truncated or disfigured—fragments of a broken vision.

In the thirties, a few "topical" films allowed the grim reality of the Depression to seep into the movies, particularly at Warner Bros. Young Darryl Zanuck, then head of production, ordered his writers to draw their subjects from newspaper headlines. *I'm a Fugitive from a Chain Gang* was probably the most famous of these hard-hitting exposés. It even led to the reformation of the penal system in the South.

However, David Selznick at RKO jumped the gun on Zanuck by releasing his own indictment of the chain-gang system several months earlier. The film was called *Hell's Highway*. It was one of the three pictures directed by Rowland Brown, a forgotten figure whose meteoric career reputedly ended when he punched one of Hollywood's top executives.

A convicted bank robber, Richard Dix is one of the "forgotten men" of the Depression. His rebellious behavior is justified by the appalling

Hell's Highway (1932): A World War I veteran becomes a bank robber
in Rowland Brown's audacious indictment of the chain-gang system.

conditions at the prison camp. And his desperation reflects that of the country. The World War I
veteran was once an all-American hero. Somehow
Rowland Brown's audacity epitomized the pre-
Code era. Those were the tumultuous years
before rigid censorship rules known as the
Production Code came into effect.

Social consciousness also sparked Warner
Bros.' stark dramas, films like William Wellman's
Wild Boys of the Road and *Heroes for Sale*. *Wild
Boys of the Road* was a movie about teenagers

who were forced to leave home to find work
because their parents had lost their jobs in the
Depression. Railroad dicks constantly harassed
and abused the teenagers. The social and political context was painted in rather broad strokes,
but the dramas were contemporary, urgent, and
gripping. "Wild Bill" Wellman had a natural
feeling for the vagabond life, for the homeless
youngsters and their battles with the authorities.
The director's sympathy lay with the outcasts
and rebels.

Wild Boys of the Road (1933): In Wellman's gripping movie, Dorothy Coonan and Frankie
Darro are teenagers forced to leave home and look for work during the Depression.

SCENE: **TEENAGE HOBOES**

In an open box car, a runaway girl, Sally (Dorothy Coonan), tells her story to two young hoboes, Eddie (Frankie Darro) and Tommy (Edwin Phillips), who are riding the rails across the country.

Sally: So I had to get to my aunt's in Chicago some way. And this is the only way I can do it.

Eddie: Well, don't your folks mind?

Sally: My mother's dead. And we got a big family. With me gone, it means just one less mouth to feed. That's why they were kinda glad to see me go.

WILLIAM WELLMAN: *WILD BOYS OF THE ROAD* (1933)

MARTIN SCORSESE At the opposite end of the spectrum, you found a different breed of iconoclasts: baroque stylists such as Josef von Sternberg. Like Stroheim, Sternberg demanded total control over all aspects of his productions. But his was a voluptuous, dreamlike, supremely artificial world, lovingly composed on the Paramount sound stages. Sternberg's radical stylization proved as provocative as Stroheim's extreme realism. Each film became a ceremonial, with the director orchestrating the most elaborate erotic rituals around his star, Marlene Dietrich.

SCENE: **SEXUAL POLITICS**

Catherine (Marlene Dietrich) surrenders to the most handsome and powerful man of the court, Count Alexei (John Lodge).

Catherine: The woman you adore is quite close to you, isn't she?

Alexei: Catherine, I worship you.

(As he embraces her passionately, they are partially hidden by the bed's thin lace curtain. We see Catherine's hand grab the lace. Preparing for the night, Alexei blows one of the candles. Catherine lies down, but he is not the one on her mind.)

Catherine: Behind the mirror, as you know, there is a flight of stairs. Down below, someone is waiting to come up. Would His Excellency be kind enough to open the door for him carefully so that he can sneak in? *(Obediently, Alexei blows out the remaining candles and slowly exits. His jealousy seems to be reflected by the statue against which he is framed: the tortured figure of Saint Sebastian.)*

JOSEF VON STERNBERG: *THE SCARLET EMPRESS* (1934)

MARTIN SCORSESE Of the seven films Sternberg made with Dietrich, *The Scarlet Empress* was the most baroque and the boldest in its depiction of erotic manipulation as it traced the transformation of an innocent Prussian princess into Catherine the Great, the Empress of Russia. As the heroine quickly discovered, political power and sexual power were inseparable. Her battles were waged in the bedroom, as she learnt the art of choosing and changing lovers at the right time. Catherine showed such considerable skills that she even challenged traditional sexual roles.

Nothing escaped Sternberg's artistic control. He wrote the script, conceived the lighting, composed some of the music, directed the Los Angeles Symphony Orchestra, helped design the sets and sculptures, and probably selected every icon himself. He even claimed that Marlene was just another tool: "Remember that Marlene is not Marlene. I'm Marlene, she knows that better than anyone." To the artist, insisted Sternberg, the subject is incidental and only his vision matters. As he put it: "The camera is a diabolical instrument that conveys ideas with lightning speed. Each picture transliterates a thousand words."

Perhaps the greatest iconoclast of them all was also the youngest: Orson Welles. He was 25 when he landed in Hollywood. In the wake of his radio show, *War of the Worlds*, the young prodigy was given unprecedented latitude by

The Scarlet Empress (1934): Marlene Dietrich in Josef von Sternberg's baroque
tale about Catherine the Great's sexual manipulation of political power.

Citizen Kane (1941): Orson Welles moved his camera in startling ways to create this revolutionary film.

Kane: . . . the downright villainy of Boss Jim W. Gettys' political machine now in complete control . . .
(Camera dollies up toward Kane in a straight, irresistible movement across the convention floor.)
Kane: I made no campaign promises. Because until a few weeks ago, I had no hope of being elected.
(Crowd laughs and applauds.)
Kane: Now, however, I have something more than a hope. And Jim Gettys . . . Jim Gettys has something less than a chance!
(Tremendous applause. On the balcony, we recognize Leland played by Joseph Cotten. In a box, we see Emily, played by Ruth Warrick, and her son, Junior. She motions, he sits down by her. More applause is heard. In another box, Gettys, played by Ray Collins, is looking down at Kane. A roar from the crowd is heard. A disgusted Gettys puts on his hat and exits.)
ORSON WELLES: *CITIZEN KANE* (1941)

RKO, including what is known today as the right to final cut. At the time, only Charlie Chaplin had such creative control over his productions.

For his first film, Welles set out to explore the many facets of media baron William Randolph Hearst, whose abuse of wealth and power defied America's democratic traditions. Some in Hollywood were so incensed that they put pressure on RKO to destroy the negative. Fortunately, they didn't succeed.

SCENE: ENCHANTED BY HIS OWN MAGIC

At Madison Square Garden, under his own banner, Kane attacks political boss Jim Gettys.

MARTIN SCORSESE Welles was like a young magician enchanted by his own magic. In fact, the most revolutionary aspect of *Citizen Kane* was its self-consciousness. The style drew attention to itself. This contradicted the classical ideal of the invisible camera and seamless cuts. Welles used every narrative technique and filmic device: deep focus, high and low angles, wide angle lenses. "I want to use the motion picture camera as an instrument of poetry," he said. And somehow Welles's passion for the medium became the great excitement of the piece itself.

ORSON WELLES (1970) You see, I had the best contract anybody has ever had for *Kane*. Nobody comes on the set. Nobody gets to look at the rushes. Nothing! You just make the picture and that's it. If I hadn't had that contract, they would have stopped me at the beginning just by the nature of the script. But it was such conditions!

The Magnificent Ambersons (1942): Welles lost control over this film (above, Tim Holt and Dolores Costello), which was edited and changed by the studio without his consent.

I've never had anything remotely equal to that contract since. So it isn't just the success. What spoiled me is having had the joy of that kind of liberty once in my life and never having been able to enjoy it again.

MARTIN SCORSESE Orson Welles inspired more would-be directors than any other filmmaker since D. W. Griffith. Yet Welles didn't change the status of the Hollywood director. He actually lost all his privileges a year after Citizen Kane on The Magnificent Ambersons, which was chopped down and even partially reshot in his absence.

ORSON WELLES (1970) Do you know that I always liked Hollywood very much? It just wasn't reciprocated.

MARTIN SCORSESE Throughout his career, Welles pushed the creative envelope in so many ways. To trace Kane's political ambitions, for instance, he created fake newsreel footage. And to give it the appropriate look, he had editor Robert Wise drag the film across a concrete floor. This was an opportunity for Welles to recall William Randolph Hearst's fondness for dictators: you saw Kane posing with Hitler for the photographers.

At the same time, in his first talking picture, Charlie Chaplin dared to aim at the fascist powers directly. At the risk of infuriating America's isolationist forces, he took on the dictators singlehandedly. A comedy drawing on such topical horrors as racial persecutions and concentration camps, *The Great Dictator* presented Chaplin with another major challenge: he gave himself a double role, that of the monster, dictator Hynkel and the victim, the Jewish barber.

Of course, even the renegades like Charlie Chaplin and Orson Welles had to work around the censors. The content of American films was still strictly controlled. Adult themes and images were too often curtailed or suppressed. But after World War II, audiences wanted pictures to be truer to life. A few of our filmmakers started challenging the rules. Elia Kazan led the assault against the censors. His *Streetcar Named Desire* caused the first major breach in Hollywood's Production Code.

Kazan fought tooth and nail, frame by frame, to preserve the integrity of Tennessee Williams's drama when he adapted it to the screen. This meant exposing the overtly carnal desires of Stanley and his battered, pregnant wife, Stella. However, several close shots of Kim Hunter could not be included in the film as it was originally released, because the Legion of Decency objected to their sensuality. The studio decided to cut them and replaced the jazz score with more conventional music.

ELIA KAZAN (1981) The camera is more than a recorder, it's a microscope. It penetrates, it goes into people and you see their most private and concealed thoughts. I have been able to do that with actors. I have revealed things that actors didn't even know they were revealing about themselves.

SCENE: **CONCEALED THOUGHTS**

In a park Terry Malloy (Marlon Brando) courts Edie Doyle (Eva Marie Saint). He is wearing one of her gloves, which he picked up earlier when she dropped it.
Terry: You know, I've seen you a lot of times before. Remember, parochial school down at Paluski Street. Seven, eight years ago, your hair, you had your hair...
Edie: Braids.
Terry: Looked like a hunk of rope. You had wires on your teeth and glasses, everything . . . *(He puts a chewing gum into his mouth.)* You was really a mess. *(She reacts and removes her glove from his hand.)*
Terry: Aw, don't get sore, I was just kiddin' you a little bit. I just mean to tell ya that you grew up very nice.
ELIA KAZAN: *ON THE WATERFRONT* (1954)

MARTIN SCORSESE I was 12 years old when I saw *On the Waterfront*. It was a breakthrough for me. Kazan was forging a new acting style. It had the appearance of realism. But actually it revealed something in the natural behavior of people that I hadn't seen on the screen before: the truth behind the posture. "Brando," Kazan observed, "was the only actor I can describe as a genius. He had that ambivalence that I believe is essential in depicting humanity, both strength and sensibility."

SCENE: **THE TRUTH BEHIND THE POSTURE**

Terry (Marlon Brando) knocks on the door of Edie's apartment (Eva Marie Saint).

A Streetcar Named Desire (1951): Kazan fought vigorously against the
censors to keep the sensual scenes of Marlon Brando and Kim Hunter.

On the Waterfront (1954): Kazan forged a new acting style in this movie. His camera reveals the innermost thoughts of Eva Marie Saint and Marlon Brando.

Terry *(off-screen)*: Edie? Edie!?

Edie: Stay away from me!

(Wearing her night slip, Edie goes to the door to lock it. She then runs back to bed. He breaks the door open. She covers her body with the sheets.)

Edie *(from her bed)*: I want you to stay away from me!

Terry: I know what you want me to do, but I ain't gonna do it, so forget it!

Edie *(getting out of bed)*: I don't want you to do anything. You let your conscience tell you what to do.

Terry: Shut up about that conscience. That's all I have been hearin'.

Edie: I never mentioned the word before. You must stay away from me!

Terry: Edie, you . . . Edie, you love me.

Edie *(facing him)*: I didn't say I didn't love you. I said, stay away from me!

Terry: I want you to say it to me . . .

Edie: Stay away from me!

(He grabs her arm and kisses her. She stops resisting when they embrace. Together they slide to the ground.)

ELIA KAZAN: *ON THE WATERFRONT* (1954)

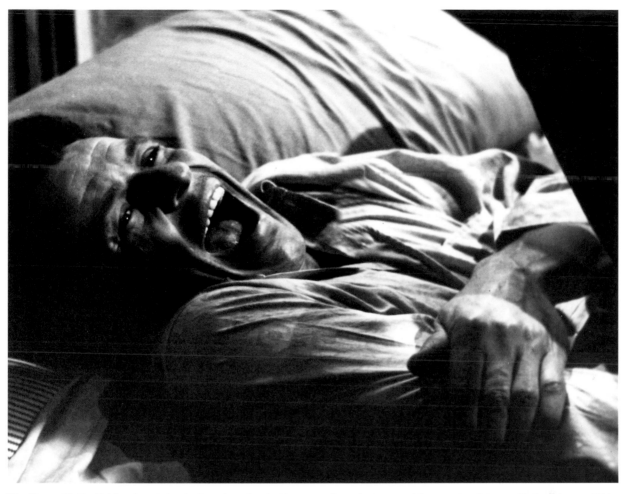

The Man with the Golden Arm (1955): Preminger's relentless crusade against censorship scored a victory with the release of this frank depiction of the horrors of drug addiction, in which Frank Sinatra plays a heroin addict.

MARTIN SCORSESE Elia Kazan paved the way for the iconoclasts of the fifties and sixties. They were writer-directors and writer-producers—men like Robert Aldrich, Richard Brooks, Robert Rossen, Billy Wilder, and, among the younger generation, Arthur Penn and Sam Peckinpah. They all defied the guardians of public morality by daring to tackle controversial issues like racism *(Apache)*, inner-city violence *(Blackboard Jungle)*, juvenile delinquency *(The Wild One)*, homosexuality *(Advise and Consent)*, war atrocities *(Paths of Glory)*, and the death penalty *(I Want to Live)*. A new reality was hitting the screens!

Producer-director Otto Preminger did more than anyone else to bring about the demise of the Production Code. His crusade against censorship led him from *The Moon is Blue*, a comedy about "professional virgins," to *Advise and Consent*, which exposed political corruption in Washington and even showed gay bars. He was also among the first to challenge the black lists by hiring Dalton Trumbo, one of the Hollywood

Ten, to write *Exodus*. One of Preminger's most important victories was scored when he made *The Man with the Golden Arm*, probably the first honest depiction of drug addiction on American screens. Frank Sinatra offered one of his most memorable performances as a heroine addict going through withdrawal.

Alexander Mackendrick's *Sweet Smell of Success* exposed a different kind of addiction—the addiction to power. The arena was Broadway, with Burt Lancaster portraying J. J. Hunsecker, the master manipulator. In Clifford Odets and Ernest Lehman's screenplay, the formidable newspaper and radio columnist was to show-business what Senator McCarthy was to Cold War politics. J. J.'s power was based on a network of informers and sycophants. His fear and intimidation tactics made him a national institution, but his ruthless world flickered in a moral twilight.

SCENE: **A MORAL TWILIGHT**

J.J. Hunsecker (Burt Lancaster) is a powerful Broadway columnist, and his side-kick, Sidney Falco (Tony Curtis), a cynical publicity agent. At his favorite restaurant, Hunsecker grills a philandering Senator (William Forrest), his mistress, and her agent Manny (Jay Adler).

J.J. Hunsecker: Manny, tell me, what exactly are the unseen gifts of this lovely young thing that you manage.

Manny: Well, she sings a little, you know, she sings and . . .

Girl *(interrupting):* Manny's faith in me is simply awe-inspiring, Mr. Hunsecker. Actually, I'm still studying.

J.J.: What subject?

Girl: Singing, of course. Straight concert and . . .

J.J.: Why "of course"? You might for instance be studying politics.

Girl: Uh, me?

Manny: Well, you see, J.J., she . . .

Girl *(overlapping):* I mean, I, you must be kidding, Mr. Hunsecker. Me with my Jersey City brains.

(Lester, a publicist, stops by the table.)

J.J. *(to Lester):* I know, that wonder boy of yours opens at the Latin Quarter next week.

Lester: J. J., I . . .

J.J.: Say goodbye, Lester . . .

J.J. *(turns to Sidney Falco, who is sitting next to him):* That's the only reason the poor slobs pay you, to see their names in my column all over the world. Now I make it out, you're doing me a favor.

Falco: I didn't say that . . .

J.J.: The day I can't get along without a press agent's handouts, I'll close up shop and move to Alaska, lock, stock and barrel.

Manny: Sweep out my igloo, here I come.

J.J.: Look, Manny, you rode in here on the Senator's shirttails, so shut your mouth!

Senator: Now come, J. J., that's a little too harsh. Anyone seems fair game for you tonight.

J.J.: This man is not for you, Harvey. And you shouldn't be seen in public with him. Because that's another part of a press agent's life. They dig up scandal about prominent people and shovel it thin among columnists who give them space.

Senator: There seems to be some allusion here that escapes me.

J.J.: We're friends, Harvey. We go as far back as when you were a fresh kid congressman, don't we?

Senator: Why is it that everything you say sounds like a threat?

J.J.: Maybe it's a mannerism, because I don't threaten friends. But why furnish your enemies with ammunition? You're a family man, Harvey, and someday, God willin', you may want to be President. And here you are, out in the open, where any hip person knows, that this one is toting that one around for you. *(The camera pans from Manny to the girl.)* Are we kids or what? *(Getting up)* Next time you come up, you might join

Sweet Smell of Success (1957): Burt Lancaster plays a manipulative show business columnist whose power is feared across the country. A McCarthy-like figure, he is seen here humiliating everyone at his table.

me on my TV show.

(The group is now standing by the table.)

Senator: Thanks, J. J., for what I consider sound advice.

J.J.: Go now and sin no more.

(He turns and leaves the group.)

ALEXANDER MACKENDRICK: *SWEET SMELL OF SUCCESS* (1957)

MARTIN SCORSESE Let's not forget that comedies can be just as iconoclastic as dramas. Billy Wilder's work, first as a writer in the thirties, then as a writer-director from the forties on, is a perfect example. Over the years, Wilder's wit only grew more abrasive. Instead of sweetening his brews, he kept adding more acid. You won't find a more iconoclastic film in the Kennedy years than his *One, Two, Three*, a savage political farce that dared ridicule all ideologies at the height of the Cold War. James Cagney plays an American Coca-Cola executive who has enrolled his German secretary to hoodwink the Soviet commissars in East Berlin.

The American manager of a Coca-Cola subsidiary, MacNamara (James Cagney) joins the Russian commissars (Leon Askin, Peter Capell, Ralph Wolter) in a Berlin tavern. He is accompanied by his curvaceous secretary Ingeborg (Lilo Pulver).

MacNamara *(shaking their hands)*: If it isn't my old friends, Hart, Schaffner, and Karl Marx.

Marx: I see you bring blonde lady with you.

Hart: Ring a ding ding.

(Marx pats Ingeborg's behind as she sits down.)

Schaffner: To what do we owe this unexpected pleasure?

MacNamara: Well, you're the trade commission, I thought we might trade.

Schaffner: Coca-Cola?

MacNamara: No, but I hear you boys would like Fraulein Ingeborg to go to work for ya.

(Ingeborg waves to the commissars.)

Schaffner: You want to trade your secretary?

MacNamara: Right.

Schaffner: For Russian secretary.

MacNamara: Oh . . .

Hart: I do not blame you. Ours is built like a bow-legged samovar! *(His hands suggest the silhouette of a squat woman. Ingeborg cracks up. The three Russians laugh too.)*

Schaffner: We find proposition very interesting. Now, what can we offer you?

MacNamara: Actually, all I want from you is a small favor.

Schaffner: Small favor, big favor, anything . . .

MacNamara: There's a guy named Otto Ludwig Piffl. He's being held by East German police.

Schaffner: For what reason?

MacNamara: Son of a gun stole my cuckoo clock.

Schaffner: You want cuckoo clock back?

MacNamara: Wrong.

Schaffner: You want Piffl back.

MacNamara: Right.

Schaffner: Impossible, my friend. We cannot interfere with internal affairs of sovereign Republic of East Germany.

MacNamara *(getting up)*: No pickle, no deal. Let's go, Ingeborg.

Schaffner: Wait! What is the hurry? You're not giving us a chance! Is old Russian proverb, "You cannot milk cow with hands in pocket." Herr Robert! *(Clasps hands.)* Vodka! Caviar! Herr Kappelmeister *(Clasps hands again.)* More rock 'n' roll!

BILLY WILDER: *ONE, TWO, THREE* (1961)

MARTIN SCORSESE Wilder's transgressions of political correctness matched his transgressions of good taste. To Wilder, "good taste" was another name for censorship: "I'm accused of being vulgar," he would say. "So much the better. That proves I'm closer to life."

BILLY WILDER The picture was hit by the change in attitude. The Wall was built. Nobody could get through, East Berlin to West Berlin, and vice versa. The desire of the audience to laugh was gone. About 25 years later, it became a smash hit in Germany. Everybody went to see it because the Wall was practically gone. It became a kind of historic vignette of the silliness of the Russians and the stupidity of the Americans.

By the late sixties, the Production Code was almost defunct. Arthur Penn, with *Bonnie and Clyde* (page 156), and Sam Peckinpah, with *The Wild Bunch*, put the nail in the coffin.

ARTHUR PENN The old studio system was so hypocritical. They were constantly fearful of being accused of instilling in youth the glory of the outlaw. So they had these rules that you couldn't even fire a gun in the same frame with

One, Two, Three (1961). Wilder's wit is savage in this political farce about the Cold War. An American Coca-Cola executive recruits his German secretary (Lilo Pulver) to deceive Soviet commissars (named Hart, Schaffner, and Karl Marx).

somebody getting hit. You had to have literally a film cut in-between.

So I thought that if we are going to show this, we should show it. We should show what it looks like when somebody gets shot. That shooting somebody is not a sanitized event, it is not immaculate. There's an enormous amount of blood, there's . . . a horror of change that takes place when that occurs. And we were in the middle of the Vietnamese War. What you saw on television every night was every bit as, perhaps even more, bloody than what we were showing on film.

MARTIN SCORSESE Today, the violence in films is certainly more graphic than it has ever been. The last frontier may be sexuality—and beyond sexuality, the complexity of the human psyche. This is the territory that Stanley Kubrick has been mining in his films.

Like Kazan, Kubrick was a New York maverick who grew into an iconoclast. He emerged from independent production and film noir to create his own unique, visionary worlds. His association with Kirk Douglas on *Paths of Glory* and *Spartacus* established him as a major player.

Bonnie and Clyde (1967): Penn's movie (starring Faye Dunaway and Warren Beatty), with its graphic depiction of violence, was one of the final assaults on the Production Code.

But he couldn't stand being an "employee" on studio projects and moved to London to make *Lolita*. He stayed there and hasn't worked in Hollywood since. He is one of the rare iconoclasts who has enjoyed the luxury of operating completely on his own terms.

THE DECISIVE FACTOR

Charlotte Haze (Shelley Winters) gives a tour of her house to Professor Humbert Humbert (James Mason), a distinguished-looking foreigner looking for a room to rent.

Charlotte: Uh, back here, we have the kitchen. That's where we have our informal meals.

Humbert: Perhaps, if you would . . .

Charlotte: My pastries win prizes around here.

Humbert: Perhaps, if you would let me have your phone number. That would give me a chance to think it over.

(Charlotte leads Humbert toward the garden.)

Charlotte: Oh, you must see the garden before you go. You must!

(Lolita, played by Sue Lyon, is in a bikini, lying in the sun, listening to loud popular music on the radio.)

Charlotte *(off-screen)*: My flowers win prizes around here. They're the talk of the neighborhood.

Charlotte: Voilà!

(Humbert is hypnotized by Lolita who is staring at him with an enigmatic smile.)

Charlotte's voice *(off-screen)*: My yellow roses. My uh, oh, my daughter. Uh, darling, turn that down, please. I can offer you a comfortable home, a sunny garden, a congenial atmosphere, my cherry pies.

(Lolita removes her dark glasses to take a better look at the professor.)

Humbert: We haven't discussed uh, how much.

Charlotte: Oh, something nominal, let's say uh, two hundred a month.

Humbert: Yes, that's very, uh . . .

Charlotte: Including meals . . . and uh, late snacks, etc. *(Quiet laugh.)*

Humbert: Yes, you're a very persuasive salesman, Mrs. Haze.

Charlotte: Thank you. Uh, what was the decisive factor? Uh, my garden?

Humbert *(avoiding Lolita's gaze)*: I think it was your cherry pies.

(Charlotte laughs off screen.)

STANLEY KUBRICK: *LOLITA* (1962)

MARTIN SCORSESE When Kubrick made *Lolita*, the subject of a middle-aged man infatuated with a sexually precocious minor was still completely taboo. This was not the contraband of a smuggler, but open defiance.

James Mason is cast as Professor Humbert Humbert, a European intellectual discovering the trappings of small-town America. His fall befits his transgression. Obsessed with Lolita, who soon runs away from him, he undergoes a mental breakdown. The satirical comedy turns into a bizarre tragedy.

SCENE: "IT WAS A DATE"

Humbert is painting Lolita's toenails in her room. She is sipping from a bottle of Coca-Cola.

Humbert: Why were you so late coming home from school yesterday afternoon?

Lolita: Yesterday? Yesterday, what was yesterday?

Humbert: Yesterday was Thursday.

Lolita: That's right, that's right. Michelle and I stayed to watch football practice.

Humbert: In the Frigid Queen?

Lolita: What do you mean, in the Frigid Queen?

Humbert: I was driving around and I thought I saw you through the window.

Lolita: Oh, yeah, well we stopped there for a malt afterwards. What difference does it make?

Lolita (1962): Kubrick defiantly dramatizes a forbidden subject: the infatuation of a middle-aged man (James Mason) for a sexually-precocious minor (Sue Lyon).

Humbert: You were sitting at a table with two boys. I told you no dates.

Lolita: It wasn't a date.

Humbert: It was a date.

Lolita: It wasn't a date.

Humbert: It was a date, Lolita.

Lolita: It was not a date.

Humbert: It was a date.

Lolita: It wasn't a date.

Humbert: Well, whatever it was that you had yesterday afternoon, I don't want you to have it again. And while we're on the subject, how did you come to be so late on Saturday afternoon?

STANLEY KUBRICK: *LOLITA* (1962)

SCENE: **AFTER THE FALL**

At the hospital, an agitated Humbert learns that Lolita has gone. He is tackled and brought under control by the nurses.

Doctor: Let's get this straight. This girl was officially discharged earlier tonight in the care of her uncle.

Humbert *(lying on his back)*: If you say so.

Doctor: Well, has she or hasn't she an uncle?

Humbert: Well, all right, let's say she has an uncle.

Doctor: What do you mean, let's say she has an uncle?

Humbert: All right, she has an uncle. Uncle Gus. And, yes, I remember now. She . . . he was going to, to, to pick her up here at the hospital. I forgot that.

Doctor: Forgot?

Humbert: Yes, I forgot.

Doctor: All right. Let him up. *(The orderlies help Humbert to his feet. As he is led out, Humbert turns back).* Uh, she didn't by any chance leave a message for me? No, I suppose not.

STANLEY KUBRICK: *LOLITA* (1962)

MARTIN SCORSESE Kubrick's boldest project was a period piece set in 18th-century Europe, *Barry Lyndon* (page 162). He broke new technical ground, having special lenses manufactured to capture the glow of the candlelit mansions of the aristocracy. Instead of a picaresque tale, though, he offered another grim journey of self-destruction, the rise and fall of an opportunist. On the surface, the approach was cool and distant—deceptive. But I have found this to be one of the most emotional films I have ever seen. Kubrick's style was strangely unsettling. His audacity was to insist on slowness in order to recreate the pace of life and the ritualized behavior of the time. A good example is the seduction scene between Ryan O'Neal and Marisa Berenson which he stretches until it settles into a sort of trance. What has always struck me is the ballet of emotions. The tension between the camera movements and the characters' body language orchestrated by music is mesmerizing.

With John Cassavetes' characters, the emotion was always upfront. It was at once their cross and their salvation. John's approach was warm, embracing, focused on people. Relationships were all he was interested in—the laughter and the games, the tears and the guilt. The whole roller coaster of love. In *Faces*, a middle-class housewife, in despair over the failure of her marriage, is picked up by a young man. She takes him home for the night. The next morning, he finds her comatose.

SCENE: **THE TEARS OF LIFE**

Chet (Seymour Cassel) finds that Lynn (Lynn Carlin) has overdosed on sleeping pills. He fails to revive her. He runs to the phone.

Chet: Operator, I want the emergency rescue squad. My number is *(He hesitates and hangs up)* . . .

(Later, Chet holds Lynn under the shower, trying to spill coffee into her mouth.)

Chet: C'mon, now, drink this, damn it. Godamn bitch,

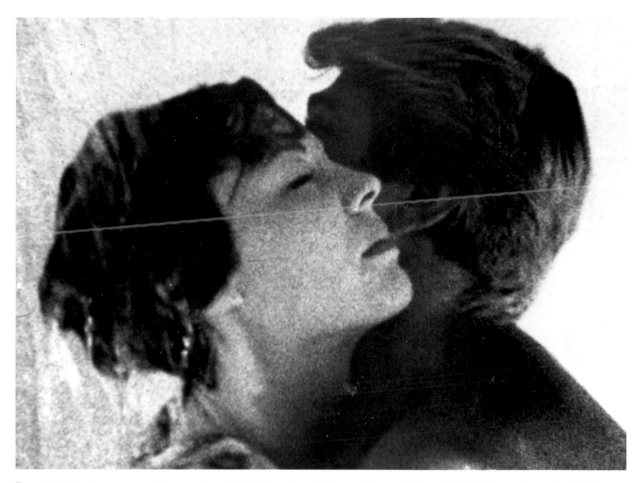

Faces (1968): A young man (Seymour Cassel) tries to revive middle-aged housewife (Lynn Carlin). Desperate over her failed marriage, she had picked up Cassel the night before and then took an overdose of pills.

drink this. C'mon, now, don't go back out . . .

(Chet carries Lynn still unconscious into the bedroom.)

Chet: No, you've got to stay awake. Please. I don't want you to die. Please, Lynn. You gotta stay awake. (He slaps her.) You gotta stay awake. (Slaps her again.) You gotta stay awake. (Slaps her again.) . . .

(Chet laughs excitedly as she starts responding when he forces her to open her eyes.)

Chet: Oh, you're gonna cry! Oh good, good! C'mon. I didn't want to hit you, but don't go to sleep on me. Oh, c'mon now, cry. That's it, that's life, honey! Tears, tears of happiness, man. Just do it! Yes, you silly nut!

(She starts crying on his shoulder . . .)

Chet: You want some coffee? Can I trust you? Huh? Huh? Okay, where are they, 'cause I don't trust you anyway. (He takes the bottle of pills.)

Aw . . . Huh! You little sneaky you, I'm gonna get you some coffee!

(Jubilant, he cavorts out of the bedroom.)

JOHN CASSAVETES: *FACES* (1968)

MARTIN SCORSESE Cassavetes embodied the emergence of a new school of guerrilla filmmaking in New York. His films were literally made on the

Barry Lyndon (1975): Kubrick had special lenses made to create the candlelight glow of Thackeray's 18th-century Europe. But under the sumptuous color and trance-like pace of this scene (Marisa Berenson facing Ryan O'Neal), the director reveals an emotional story of self-destruction.

credit plan. John was fearless—a true renegade setting up one psychodrama after another with the complicity of a close group of actor friends. He insisted on having "fun" when making films—while looking for some kind of truth, maybe even a "revelation."

JOHN CASSAVETES (1984) To have a philosophy is to know how to love and to know where to put it. You can't put it everywhere. You gotta be a priest saying, "Yes, my son, or yes, my daughter, bless you." But people don't live that way. They live with anger and hostility and problems. And lack of money, you know, tremendous disappointments in their life. So what they need is a philosophy. What I think everybody needs is a way to say, "Where and how can I love and be in love so that I can live with some degree of peace?" So that's why I have a need for the characters to really analyze love, discuss it, kill it,

Faces (1968): In this deceptively primitive black-and-white image of Lynn Carlin, Cassavetes shows the whole gamut of love. Made with little money and a close group of actor friends, his films put the emotion up front while searching for the "truth" in the human face.

destroy it, hurt each other, do all that stuff, in that war, that word polemic and picture polemic of what life is. And the rest of the stuff really doesn't interest me. It may interest other people, but I have a one-track mind. That's all I'm interested in. It's love.

MARTIN SCORSESE All of Cassavetes' films were "epics of the human soul." Watching them brings to mind a comment made by John Ford to a collaborator who was complaining about the miserable weather conditions when they were trying to shoot a picture in the desert. The man asked: "Look, Mr. Ford, what can we shoot out here?" And Ford replied: "What can we shoot? The most interesting and exciting thing in the whole world, a human face."

CONCLUSION

MARTIN SCORSESE This is where we have got to stop. We just don't have the time and space to go on any further. Also, we have reached a different era, the late sixties, the years when I started making movies myself. This is a whole new chapter altogether. And it puts me in a different perspective. I could not really do justice to my friends who are making films, my companions, my generation of filmmakers. Not from the inside.

This story really has no end. We haven't even started discussing such major figures as Ernst Lubitsch, Preston Sturges, Joseph Mankiewicz, John Huston, George Stevens, Sam Peckinpah, William Wyler, and of course Alfred Hitchcock. Fortunately, they have been celebrated in so many ways elsewhere: books, articles and some wonderful shows. Documentaries about film are becoming a genre in themselves thanks to Kevin Brownlow and David Gill's invaluable 13-hour series about Hollywood's silent era, to Peter Bogdanovich's essay *Directed by John Ford,* to Richard Schickel's series *The Men Who Made the Movies,* and so many British and French portraits of filmmakers.

So many directors have inspired me over the years. I wouldn't know where to start if I had to name them all: Tod Browning, Fred Zinnemann, Leo McCarey, Henry King, James Whale, Robert Wise, Gregory La Cava, Donald Siegel, Roger Corman, Jean Renoir. We are indebted to them, as we are to any original filmmaker who managed to survive and impose his or her vision in a very competitive profession.

When we talk about personal expression, I'm often reminded of Kazan's *America America,* the story of his uncle's journey from Anatolia to America, the story of so many immigrants who came to this country from a distant foreign land. I kind of identified with it. I was very moved by it. Actually, I later saw myself making the same journey, not from Anatolia, but rather from my own neighborhood in New York, which was in a

The Spiritual Side of Man: Jimmy Stewart carrying Kim Novak in Alfred Hitchcock's *Vertigo*

sense a very foreign land. My journey took me from that land to moviemaking—which was something unimaginable!

In fact, when I was a little younger, there was another journey I wanted to make: a religious one. I wanted to be a priest. However, I soon realized that my real vocation, my real calling, was the movies. I don't really see a conflict between the church and the movies, the sacred and the profane. Obviously, there are major differences, but I can also see great similarities between a church and a movie house. Both are

places for people to come together and share a common experience. I believe there is a spirituality in films, even if it's not one which can supplant faith. I find that over the years many films address themselves to the spiritual side of man's nature, from Griffith's *Intolerance* to John Ford's *The Grapes of Wrath*, to Hitchcock's *Vertigo*, to Kubrick's *2001* . . . and so many more. It is as though movies answered an ancient quest for the common unconscious. They fulfill a spiritual need that people have to share a common memory.

FILMOGRAPHY

Filmography

All That Heaven Allows

(DOUGLAS SIRK, 1955)

Sc.: Peg Fenwick, from a story by Edna Lee and Harry Lee. *Ph.:* Russell Metty (Technicolor). *Mus.:* Frank Skinner, Joseph Gershenson. *Prod.:* Ross Hunter (Universal-International). *Cast:* Jane Wyman, Rock Hudson, Agnes Moorehead, Conrad Nagel, Virginia Grey, Gloria Talbot, William Reynolds. *

All That Jazz

(BOB FOSSE, 1979)

Sc.: Robert Alan Aurthur, Bob Fosse. *Ph.:* Giuseppe Rotunno (Technicolor). *Mus.:* Ralph Burns. *Chor.:* Bob Fosse. *Prod. des.:* Philip Rosenberg, Tony Walton. *Prod.:* Daniel Melnick, Robert Alan Aurthur. (20th Century-Fox and Columbia). *Cast:* Roy Scheider, Jessica Lange, Anne Reinking, Leland Palmer, Cliff Gorman, Ben Vereen. *VHS, LD*

America, America

(ELIA KAZAN, 1963)

Sc.: Elia Kazan, from his novel. *Ph.:* Haskell Wexler. *Mus.:* Manos Hadjidakis. *Prod. des.:* Gene Callahan. *Prod.:* Elia Kazan for Athena Enterprises. *Cast:* Stathis Giallelis, Harry Davis, Frank Wolff, Elena Karam, Gregory Rozakis, John Marley, Lou Antonio, Paul Mann. *VHS*

Anna Christie

(CLARENCE BROWN, 1930)

Sc.: Frances Marion, from the play by Eugene O'Neill. *Titles:* Madeleine Ruthven. *Ph.:* William Daniels. *Prod.:* MGM. *Cast:* Greta Garbo, Charles Bickford, George F. Marion, Marie Dressler. *VHS* *

The Bad and the Beautiful

(VINCENTE MINNELLI, 1952)

Sc.: Charles Schnee, from George Bradshaw's story, "Memorial to a Bad Man." *Ph.:* Robert Surtees. *Mus.:* David Raksin. *Prod.:* John Houseman. (MGM). *Cast:* Kirk Douglas, Lana Turner, Walter Pidgeon, Dick Powell, Barry Sullivan, Gloria Grahame, Gilbert Roland, Leo G. Carroll, Paul Stewart, Ivan Triesault. *VHS, LD*

The Bandwagon

(VINCENTE MINNELLI, 1953)

Sc.: Betty Comden, Adolph Green. *Ph.:* Harry Jackson (Technicolor). *Mus.:* Arthur Schwartz. *Lyr.:* Howard Dietz. *Chor.:* Fred Astaire, Michael Kidd. *Ass. prod.:* Roger Edens. *Prod.:* Arthur Freed. (MGM). *Cast:* Fred Astaire, Cyd Charisse, Oscar Levant, Nanette Fabray, Jack Buchanan. *VHS, LD*

Barry Lyndon

(STANLEY KUBRICK, 1975)

Sc.: Stanley Kubrick, from the novel by William Makepeace Thackeray. *Ph.:* John Alcott (color). *Mus.:* Leonard Rosenman. *Prod. des.:* Ken Adam. *Prod.:* Stanley Kubrick for Hawks Films LTD–Peregrine. (Warner Bros.). *Cast:* Ryan O'Neal, Marisa Berenson, Patrick Magee, Hardy Krüger, Steven Berkoff, Gay Hamilton, Marie Kean, Diana Koerner, Murray Melvin. *VHS, LD* *

Bigger Than Life

(NICHOLAS RAY, 1956)

Sc.: Cyril Hume, Richard Maibaum (and uncredited contributions by Nicholas Ray, James Mason, Gavin Lambert, Clifford Odets), from the article "Ten Feet Tall" by Berton Roueché. *Ph.:* Joe MacDonald (color by De Luxe, CinemaScope). *Mus.:* David Raksin. *Prod.:* James Mason. (20th Century-Fox). *Cast:* James Mason, Barbara Rush, Walter Matthau, Robert Simon, Christopher Olsen. *

The Big House

(GEORGE HILL, 1930)

Sc.: Frances Marion with additional dialogue by Joe Farnham and Martin Flavin. *Ph.:* Harold Wenstrom. *Prod.:* MGM. *Cast:* Chester Morris, Wallace Beery, Lewis Stone, Robert Montgomery, Leila Hyams, George F. Marion, Karl Dane. *VHS* *

The Birth of a Nation

(D. W. GRIFFITH, 1915)

Sc.: D. W. Griffith, Frank E. Woods, Thomas Dixon, from *The Clansman* and *The Leopard's Spots* by Thomas Dixon. *Ph.:* Billie Bitzer. *Cam.:* Karl Brown. *Mus.:* Joseph Carl Breil, D. W. Griffith. *Asst. dir.:* Elmer Clifton, Erich von Stroheim, Raoul Walsh. *Prod.:* D. W. Griffith for Epoch Producing Corporation. *Cast:* Henry B. Walthall, Lillian Gish, Mae Marsh, Miriam Cooper, Mary Alden, Ralph Lewis, George Siegmann, Walter Long, Robert Harron, Elmer Clifton, Donald Crisp, Raoul Walsh. *VHS, LD*

Bonnie and Clyde

(ARTHUR PENN, 1967)

Sc.: David Newman, Robert Benton. *Ph.:* Burnett Guffey (Technicolor). *Mus.:* Charles Strouse. *Prod. des.:* Dean Tavoularis. *Prod.:* Warren Beatty. (Warner Bros.). *Cast:* Warren Beatty, Faye Dunaway, Michael J. Pollard, Gene Hackman, Estelle Parsons, Denver Pyle, Gene Wilder. *VHS, LD*

Broken Blossoms

(D. W. GRIFFITH, 1919)

Sc.: D. W. Griffith, from "The Chink and the Child" in *Limehouse Nights* by Thomas Burke. *Ph.:* Billy Bitzer. *Cam.:* Karl Brown. *Mus.:* Louis F. Gottschalk, D. W. Griffith. *Prod.:* D. W. Griffith for D. W. Griffith Inc. (United Artists). *Cast:* Lillian Gish, Richard Barthelmess, Donald Crisp, Arthur Howard, Edward Peil. *VHS, LD*

The Cameraman

(EDWARD SEDGWICK, 1928)

Sc.: Richard Schayer, from a story by Clyde Bruckman, Lex Lipton. *Titl.:* Joe W. Farnham. *Ph.:* Elgin Lessley, Reggie Lanning. *Prod.:* Buster Keaton. (MGM). *Cast:* Buster Keaton, Marceline Day, Harold Goodwin, Harry Cribbon, Sidney Bracy, Edward Brothy. *VHS, LD* *

Cat People

(JACQUES TOURNEUR, 1942)

Sc.: DeWitt Bodeen, from a story by Bodeen and Val Lewton. *Ph.:* Nicholas Musuraca. *Mus.:* Roy Webb. *Ed.:* Mark Robson. *Prod.:* Val Lewton. (RKO). *Cast:* Simone Simon, Kent Smith, Tom Conway, Jane Randolph, Jack Holt, Alan Napier, Elizabeth Russell, Elizabeth Dunne. *VHS, LD* *

Citizen Kane

(ORSON WELLES, 1941)

Sc.: Herman J. Mankiewicz, Orson Welles. *Ph.:* Gregg Toland. *Mus.:* Bernard Herrmann. *Ed.:* Robert Wise. *Prod.:* Orson Welles for Mercury Productions. (RKO). *Cast:* Orson Welles, Joseph Cotten, Everett Sloane, Dorothy Comingore, Ray Collins, William Alland, Agnes Moorehead, Ruth Warrick, Paul Stewart. *VHS, LD*

Colorado Territory

(RAOUL WALSH, 1949)

Sc.: John Twist, Edmund H. North, from the novel *High Sierra* by W.R. Burnett. *Ph.:* Sid Hickox. *Mus.:* David Buttolph. *Prod.:* Anthony Veiller. (Warner Bros.). *Cast.:* Joel McCrea, Virginia Mayo, Dorothy Malone, Henry Hull, John Archer, James Mitchell, Morris Ankrum. *

Crime Wave

(ANDRÉ DE TOTH, 1954)

Sc.: Crane Wilbur, adapted by Bernard Gordon, Richard Wormser, from the *Saturday Evening Post* story "Criminal Mark" by John and Ward Hawkins. *Ph.:* Bert Glennon. *Mus.:* David Buttolph. *Prod.:* Bryan Foy. (Warner Bros.). *Cast:* Gene Nelson, Phyllis Kirk, Sterling Hayden, James Bell, Ted De Corsia, Charles Buchinsky, Ned Young, Jay Novello. *

The Crowd

(KING VIDOR, 1928)

Sc.: King Vidor, John V. A. Weaver, Harry Behn, from a story by King Vidor. *Titles:* Joseph Farnham. *Ph.:* Henry Sharp. *Prod.:* King Vidor. (MGM). *Cast:* Eleanor Boardman, James Murray, Bert Roach, Estelle Clark. *VHS, LD* *

Death's Marathon

(D. W. GRIFFITH, 1913).

Sc.: W. E. Wing. *Ph.:* Billy Bitzer. *Prod.:* Biograph. *Cast:* Blanche Sweet, Henry B. Walthall, Robert Harron, Lionel Barrymore, Alfred Paget. *

Detour

(EDGAR G. ULMER, 1946)

Sc.: Martin Goldsmith. *Ph.:* Benjamin H. Kline. *Mus.:* Leo Erdody. *Prod.:* Leon Fromkess. (PRC). *Cast:* Tom Neal, Ann Savage, Claudia Drake, Edmund MacDonald. *VHS*

Double Indemnity

(BILLY WILDER, 1944).

Sc.: Raymond Chandler, Billy Wilder, from the novel by James M. Cain. *Ph.:* John F. Seitz. *Mus.:* Miklos Rosza. *Prod.:* Buddy DeSylva, Joseph Sistrom. (Paramount). *Cast:* Fred MacMurray, Barbara Stanwyck, Edward G. Robinson, Porter Hall, Jean Heather, Tom Powers. *VHS, LD* *

Duel in the Sun

(KING VIDOR AND UNCREDITED DIRECTOR WILLIAM DIETERLE, 1946).

Sc.: David O. Selznick, from the novel by Niven Busch. *Adapt.:* Oliver H. P. Garrett. *Vis. cons.:* Josef von Sternberg. *Ph.:* Lee Garmes, Hal Rosson, Ray Rennahan (Technicolor). *Mus.:* Dimitri Tiomkin. *Prod.:* David O. Selznick for Vanguard. (S.R.O.) *Cast:* Jennifer Jones, Joseph Cotten, Gregory Peck, Lionel Barrymore, Lillian Gish, Walter Huston, Herbert Marshall, Charles Bickford, Tilly Losch, Harry Carey, and the voice of Orson Welles. *VHS*

East of Eden

(ELIA KAZAN, 1955)

Sc.: Paul Osborn, from the novel by John Steinbeck. *Ph.:* Ted McCord (Warnercolor, CinemaScope). *Mus.:* Leonard Rosenman. *Prod.:* Elia Kazan. (Warner Bros.). *Cast:* James Dean, Julie Harris, Raymond Massey, Richard Davalos, Burl Ives, Jo Van Fleet, Albert Dekker, Lois Smith, Timothy Carey, Nick Dennis. *VHS*

Faces

(JOHN CASSAVETES, 1968)

Sc.: John Cassavetes. *Ph.:* Al Ruban. *Mus.:* Jack Ackerman. *Prod.:* Maurice McEndree. *Cast:* Gena Rowlands, John Marley, Lynn Carlin, Seymour Cassel, Fred Draper, Val Avery, Dorothy Gulliver, Joanne Moore Jordan, Darlene Conley. *VHS*

The Fall of the Roman Empire

(ANTHONY MANN, 1964)

Sc.: Ben Barzman, Basilio Franchina, Philip Yordan. *Ph.:* Robert Krasker (Technicolor, Ultra Panavision 70). *Mus.:* Dimitri Tiomkin. *2nd unit dir.:* Andrew Marton, Yakima Canutt. *Prod.:* Samuel Bronston, Michael Waszynski, Jaime Prades for Samuel Bronston Productions. *Cast:* Sophia Loren, Stephen Boyd, Alec Guinness, James Mason, Christopher Plummer, Anthony Quayle, John Ireland, Mel Ferrer, Omar Sharif, Eric Porter, Douglas Wilmer, Finlay Currie. *VHS, LD*

Footlight Parade

(LLOYD BACON, 1933)

Sc.: Manuel Seff, James Seymour. *Ph.:* George Barnes. *Mus.:* Harry Warren, Sammy Fain. *Lyr.:* Al Dubin, Irving Kahal. *Chor.:* Busby Berkeley. *Prod.:* Darryl Zanuck, Robert Lord. (Warner Bros.). *Cast:* James Cagney, Joan Blondell, Ruby Keeler, Dick Powell, Guy Kibbee, Frank McHugh. *VHS, LD*

Force of Evil

(ABRAHAM POLONSKY, 1948)

Sc.: Abraham Polonsky, Ira Wolfert, from the novel *Tucker's People* by Ira Wolfert. *Ph.:* George Barnes. *Mus.:* David Raksin. *Dial. dir.:* Don Weis. *Asst. dir.:* Robert Aldrich. *Prod.:* Bob Roberts for Enterprise Studio. (MGM). *Cast:* John Garfield, Beatrice Pearson, Thomas Gomez, Marie Windsor, Roy Roberts, Howland Chamberlain, Sheldon Leonard. *VHS, LD* *

42nd Street

(LLOYD BACON, 1933)

Sc.: James Seymour, Rian James, from the novel by Bradford Ropes. *Ph.:* Sol Polito. *Mus.:* Harry Warren. *Lyr.:* Al Dubin. *Chor.:* Busby Berkeley. *Prod.:* Darryl F. Zanuck, Hal B. Wallis. (Warner Bros.). *Cast:* Warner Baxter, Bebe Daniels, George Brent, Ruby Keeler, Dick Powell, Ginger Rogers, Una Merkel, Guy Kibbee, Ned Sparks. *VHS, LD*

Forty Guns

(SAMUEL FULLER, 1957)

Sc.: Samuel Fuller. *Ph.:* Joseph Biroc (CinemaScope). *Mus.:* Harry Sukman. *Prod.:* Samuel Fuller for Globe Enterprises. (20th Century-Fox). *Cast:* Barbara Stanwyck, Barry Sullivan, Dean Jagger, John Ericson, Gene Barry, Robert Dix, Hank Worden. *

The Furies

(ANTHONY MANN, 1950)

Sc.: Charles Schnee, from a story by Niven Busch. *Ph.:* Victor Milner. *Mus.:* Franz Waxman. *Prod.:* Hal B. Wallis. (Paramount). *Cast:* Barbara Stanwyck, Wendell Corey, Walter Huston, Judith Anderson, Gilbert Roland, Thomas Gomez, Beulah Bondi, Albert Dekker, Wallace Ford, Blanche Yurka, Frank Ferguson. *

Gold Diggers of 1933

(MERVYN LEROY, 1933).

Sc.: Erwin Gelsey, James Seymour, from the Broadway play *The Gold Diggers* by Avery Hopwood. *Dial.:* David Boehm, Ben Markson. *Ph.:* Sol Polito. *Mus.:* Harry Warren. *Lyrics:* Al Dubin. *Chor.:* Busby Berkeley. *Prod.:* Robert Lord. (Warner Bros.). Cast: Warren William, Joan Blondell, Aline MacMahon, Ruby Keeler, Dick Powell, Ginger Rogers, Ned Sparks, Guy Kibbee. *VHS, LD* *

The Great Dictator

(CHARLES CHAPLIN, 1940)

Sc.: Charles Chaplin. *Ph.:* Karl Struss, Rollie Totheroh. *Mus.:* Charles Chaplin, Meredith Wilson. *Prod.:* Charles Chaplin. *Cast:* Charles Chaplin, Paulette Goddard, Jack Oakie, Reginald Gardiner, Henry Daniell, Billy Gilbert, Lucien Prival. *VHS*

The Great Train Robbery

(EDWIN S. PORTER, 1903)

Sc.: Edwin S. Porter. *Prod.:* The Edison Company. *Cast:* George Barnes, A. C. Abadie, Marie Murray, G. M. Anderson. *VHS, LD* *

Gun Crazy

(JOSEPH H. LEWIS, 1950)

Sc.: MacKinlay Kantor, Dalton Trumbo, from a *Saturday Evening Post* story by Kantor. *Ph.:* Russell Harlan. *Mus.:* Victor Young. *Prod.:* Frank and Maurice King for King Brothers. (United Artists). *Cast:* John Dall, Peggy Cummins, Berry Kroeger, Annabel Shaw, Morris Carnovsky, Nedrick Young. *VHS* *

Hell's Highway

(ROWLAND BROWN, 1932)

Sc.: Rowland Brown, Samuel Ornitz, Robert Tasker. *Ph.:* Edward Cronjager. *Mus.:* Max Steiner. *Prod.:* David O. Selznick. (RKO). *Cast:* Richard Dix, Tom Brown, Rochelle Hudson, Louise Carter, C. Henry Gordon, Oscar Apfel, Warner Richmond, Charles Middleton, John Arledge, Clarence Muse. *

Her Man

(TAY GARNETT, 1930)

Sc.: Tom Buckingham, from a story by Tay Garnett, Howard Higgin. *Ph.:* Edward Snyder. *Mus.:* Josiah Zuro. *Prod.:* E. B. Derr, Tay Garnett. (Pathé Exchange). *Cast:* Helen Twelvetrees, Marjorie Rambeau, Ricardo Cortez, Phillips Holmes, James Gleason, Harry Sweet, Franklin Pangborn, Slim Summerville. *

High Sierra

(RAOUL WALSH, 1941)

Sc.: John Huston, W. R. Burnett, from the novel by W. R. Burnett. *Ph.:* Tony Gaudio. *Mus.:* Adolph Deutsch. *Prod.:* Hal B. Wallis, Mark Hellinger. (Warner Bros.). *Cast:* Humphrey Bogart, Ida Lupino, Alan Curtis, Arthur Kennedy, Joan Leslie, Henry Hull, Henry Travers, Elizabeth Risdon, Cornel Wilde. *VHS, LD* *

Intolerance

(D. W. GRIFFITH, 1916)

Sc.: D. W. Griffith. *Ph.:* Billy Bitzer. *Cam.:* Karl Brown. *Mus.:* D. W. Griffith, Joseph Carl Breil. *Asst. dir.:* Allan Dwan, Erich von Stroheim, W. S. Van Dyke, Tod Browning, Jack Conway, George Hill, Victor Fleming. *Prod.:* D. W. Griffith for Wark Producing Corporation. *Cast:* Lillian Gish, Mae Marsh, Constance Talmadge, Margery Wilson, Robert Harron, Miriam Cooper, Walter Long, Howard Gaye, Bessie Love, George Walsh, Eugene Pallette, Elmer Clifton, Alfred Paget, Seena Owen, Tully Marshall. *VHS, LD*

I Walk Alone

(BYRON HASKIN, 1948)

Sc.: Charles Schnee, adapted by Robert Smith, John Bright, from the play *Beggars Are Coming to Town* by Theodore Reeves. *Ph.:* Leo Tover. *Mus.:* Victor Young. *Prod.:* Hal B. Wallis. (Paramount). *Cast:* Burt Lancaster, Lizabeth Scott, Kirk Douglas, Wendell Corey, George Rigaud, Marc Lawrence, Mike Mazurski. *

I Walked with a Zombie

(JACQUES TOURNEUR, 1943)

Sc.: Curt Siodmak, Ardel Wray, from an *American Weekly* story by Inez Wallace. *Ph.:* J. Roy Hunt. *Mus.:* Roy Webb. *Ed.:* Mark Robson. *Prod.:* Val Lewton. (RKO). *Cast:* Frances Dee, James Ellison, Tom Conway, Edith Barrett, Christine Gordon, James Bell, Teresa Harris, Darby Jones, Sir Lancelot. *VHS, LD* *

Johnny Guitar
(NICHOLAS RAY, 1954)

Sc.: Philip Yordan, from the novel by Roy Chanslor. *Ph.:* Harry Stradling (Trucolor). *Mus.:* Victor Young. *Prod.:* Herbert J. Yates. (Republic Pictures). *Cast:* Joan Crawford, Sterling Hayden, Mercedes McCambridge, Scott Brady, Ward Bond, Ben Cooper, Ernest Borgnine, John Carradine, Royal Dano, Frank Ferguson. *VHS* *

Kiss Me Deadly
(ROBERT ALDRICH, 1955)

Sc.: A. I. Bezzerides, from the novel by Mickey Spillane. *Ph.:* Ernest Laszlo. *Mus.:* Frank DeVol. *Prod.:* Robert Aldrich, Victor Saville for Parklane Productions. (United Artists). *Cast:* Ralph Meeker, Marion Carr, Albert Dekker, Paul Stewart, Maxine Cooper, Gaby Rodgers, Wesley Addy, Nick Dennis, Cloris Leachman, Jack Lambert, Jack Elam. *VHS, LD* *

Land of the Pharaohs
(HOWARD HAWKS, 1955)

Sc.: William Faulkner, Harry Kurnitz, Harold Jack Bloom. *Ph.:* Lee Garmes, Russell Harlan (Warnercolor, CinemaScope). *Mus.:* Dimitri Tiomkin. *2nd unit dir.:* Noel Howard. *Prod.:* Howard Hawks for Continental Productions. (Warner Bros.). *Cast:* Jack Hawkins, Joan Collins, Dewey Martin, Alexis Minotis, James Robertson Justice, Luisa Boni, Sydney Chaplin. *VHS, LD* *

Leave Her to Heaven
(JOHN M. STAHL, 1945)

Sc.: Jo Swerling, from the novel by Ben Ames Williams. *Ph.:* Leon Shamroy (Technicolor). *Mus.:* Alfred Newman. *Prod.:* William A. Bacher. (20th Century-Fox). *Cast:* Gene Tierney, Cornel Wilde, Jeanne Crain, Vincent Price, Mary Philips, Ray Collins, Gene Lockhart, Darryl Hickman, Chill Wills. *VHS, LD* *

The Left-Handed Gun
(ARTHUR PENN,1958)

Sc.: Leslie Stevens, from the teleplay *The Death of Billy the Kid* by Gore Vidal. *Ph.:* J. Peverell Marley. *Mus.:* Alexander Courage. *Prod.:* Fred Coe. (Warner Bros.). *Cast:* Paul Newman, Lita Milan, John Dehner, Hurd Hatfield, James Best. *VHS*

Letter from an Unknown Woman
(MAX OPHULS, 1948)

Sc.: Howard Koch, Max Ophuls, from the novella by Stefan Zweig. *Ph.:* Franz Planer. *Mus.:* Daniele Amfitheatrof. *Prod.:* John Houseman. (Universal-International). *Cast:* Joan Fontaine, Louis Jourdan, Mady Christians, Marcel Journet, John Good, Carol Yorke, Art Smith. *VHS, LD* *

Lolita
(STANLEY KUBRICK, 1962)

Sc.: Vladimir Nabokov, from his novel. *Ph.:* Oswald Morris. *Mus.:* Nelson Riddle. *Prod.:* James B. Harris for Seven Arts-Anya-Transworld. (MGM). *Cast:* James Mason, Shelley Winters, Peter Sellers, Sue Lyon, Marianne Stone, Diana Decker. *VHS, LD* *

The Magnificent Ambersons
(ORSON WELLES, 1942)

Sc.: Orson Welles, from the novel by Booth Tarkington (additional contributions by Jack Moss, Joseph Cotten). *Ph.:* Stanley Cortez. *Mus.:* Bernard Herrman, Roy Webb. *Ed.:* Robert Wise. (Additional scenes filmed by Freddie Fleck, Robert Wise, Jack Moss). *Prod.:* Orson Welles for Mercury Productions. (RKO). Cast: Tim Holt, Joseph Cotten, Dolores Costello, Agnes Moorehead, Anne Baxter, Ray Collins, Richard Bennett. *VHS, LD* *

The Man with the Golden Arm
(OTTO PREMINGER, 1955)

Sc.: Walter Newman, Lewis Meltzer, from the novel by Nelson Algren. *Ph.:* Sam Leavitt. *Mus.:* Elmer Bernstein. *Titl.:* Saul Bass. *Prod.:* Otto Preminger for Carlyle Productions. (United Artists). *Cast:* Frank Sinatra, Kim Novak, Eleanor Parker, Arnold Stang, Darren McGavin, Robert Strauss, George Matthews, John Conte, Doro Merande, George E. Stone, Emile Meyer. *VHS*

Meet Me in St. Louis
(VINCENTE MINNELLI, 1944)

Sc.: Irving Bretcher, Fred F. Finklehoffe, from *The New Yorker* stories and novel by Sally Benson. *Ph.:* George Folsey (Technicolor). *Mus.:* Hugh Martin, Ralph Blane. *Orch.:* Roger Edens, Conrad Salinger. *Chor.:* Charles Walters. *Prod.:* Arthur Freed. (MGM). *Cast:* Judy Garland, Margaret O'Brien, Mary Astor, Lucille Bremer, Leon Ames, Tom Drake, Marjorie Main. *VHS, LD*

Murder by Contract
(IRVING LERNER, 1958)

Sc.: Ben Simcoe. *Ph.:* Lucien Ballard. *Mus.:* Perry Botkin. *Prod.:* Leon Chooluck for Orbit Productions. (Columbia). *Cast:* Vince Edwards, Philip Pine, Herschel Bernardi, Caprice Toriel, Michael Granger. *

The Musketeers of Pig Alley
(D. W. GRIFFITH, 1912)

Sc.: D. W. Griffith. *Ph.:* Billy Bitzer. *Prod.:* Biograph. *Cast:* Elmer Booth, Alfred Paget, Lillian Gish, Walter C. Miller, Lionel Barrymore, Harry Carey, Robert Harron, Dorothy Gish. *VHS* *

My Dream is Yours
(MICHAEL CURTIZ, 1949)

Sc.: Harry Kurnitz, Dane Lurrier, from a story by Jerry Wald. *Ph.:* Ernest Haller (Technicolor). *Mus.:* Harry Warren, Ralph Blane. *Prod.:* Michael Curtiz. (Warner Bros.). *Cast:* Doris Day, Jack Carson, Lee Bowman, Adolphe Menjou, Eve Arden, S.Z. Sakall, Edgar Kennedy, Sheldon Leonard. *VHS, LD* *

The Naked Kiss
(SAMUEL FULLER, 1964)

Sc.: Samuel Fuller. *Ph.:* Stanley Cortez. *Mus.:* Paul Dunlap. *Prod.:* Samuel Fuller for Leon Fromkess–Sam Firks Productions. (Allied Artists). *Cast:* Constance Towers, Anthony Eisley, Michael Dante, Virginia Grey, Patsy Kelly. *VHS, LD*

The Naked Spur
(ANTHONY MANN, 1953).

Sc.: Sam Rolfe, Harold Jack Bloom. *Ph.:* William Mellor (Technicolor). *Mus.:* Bronislau Kaper. *Prod.:* William W. Wright. (MGM). *Cast:* James Stewart, Janet Leigh, Robert Ryan, Ralph Meeker, Millard Mitchell. *VHS, LD*

One, Two, Three
(BILLY WILDER, 1961)

Sc.: Billy Wilder, I. A. L. Diamond, from the play by Ferenc Molnar. *Ph.:* Daniel Fapp (Panavision). *Prod.:* Billy Wilder for Mirisch Company–Pyramid. (United Artists). *Cast:* James Cagney, Horst Buchholz, Pamela Tiffin, Arlene Francis, Lilo Pulver, Howard St. John, Hanns Lothar, Leon Askin, Peter Capell, Red Buttons. *VHS* *

On the Waterfront
(ELIA KAZAN, 1954)

Sc.: Budd Schulberg, from his original story based on a series of articles by Malcolm Johnson. *Ph.:* Boris Kaufman. *Mus.:* Leonard Bernstein. *Prod.:* Sam Spiegel for Horizon Films. (Columbia). *Cast:* Marlon Brando, Eva Marie Saint, Karl Malden, Lee J. Cobb, Rod Steiger, Pat Henning, James Westerfield, Leif Ericson. *VHS, LD*

Outrage
(IDA LUPINO, 1950)

Sc.: Collier Young, Malvin Wald, Ida Lupino. *Ph.:* Archie Stout. *Mus.:* Paul Sawtell. *Prod. des.:* Harry Horner. *Prod.:* Collier Young for Filmakers. (RKO). Cast: Mala Powers, Tod Andrews, Robert Clarke, Raymond Bond, Lilian Hamilton, Rita Lupino, Jerry Paris. *

The Phenix City Story

(PHIL KARLSON, 1955)

Sc.: Crane Wilbur, Daniel Mainwaring. *Ph.:* Harry Neumann. *Mus.:* Harry Sukman. *Prod.:* Samuel Bischoff, David Diamond. (Allied Artists). *Cast:* John McIntyre, Richard Kiley, Edward Andrews, Kathryn Grant, James Edwards.

Pickup on South Street

(SAMUEL FULLER, 1953)

Sc.: Samuel Fuller, from a story by Dwight Taylor. *Ph.:* Joe MacDonald. *Mus.:* Leigh Harline. *Prod.:* Jules Schermer (20th Century-Fox). *Cast:* Richard Widmark, Jean Peters, Thelma Ritter, Murvyn Vye, Richard Kiley, Willis Bouchey, George E. Stone. *VHS ***

Point Blank

(JOHN BOORMAN, 1967).

Sc.: Alexander Jacobs, David Newhouse, Rafe Newhouse, from the novel *The Hunter* by Richard Stark (aka Donald Westlake). *Ph.:* Philip H. Lathrop (Metrocolor, Panavision). *Col. cons.:* Bill Stair. *Mus.:* Johnny Mandel. *Ed.:* Henry Berman. *Prod.:* Judd Bernard, Robert Chartoff. (MGM). *Cast:* Lee Marvin, Angie Dickinson, Keenan Wynn, Carroll O'Connor, Michael Strong, John Vernon. *VHS, LD*

The Public Enemy

(WILLIAM WELLMAN, 1931)

Sc.: Kubec Glasmon, John Bright, adapted by Harvey Thew from the story "Beer and Blood" by Bright. *Ph.:* Dev Jennings. *Mus.:* David Mendoza. *Prod.:* Darryl Zanuck, Hal B. Wallis. (Warner Bros.). *Cast:* James Cagney, Jean Harlow, Edward Woods, Joan Blondell, Donald Cook, Mae Clark, Leslie Fenton, Beryl Mercer. *VHS*

Raw Deal

(ANTHONY MANN, 1948)

Sc.: Leopold Atlas, John C. Higgins, from a story by Arnold B. Armstrong and Audrey Ashley. *Ph.:* John Alton. *Mus.:* Paul Sawtell. *Prod.:* Edward Small for Edward Small Productions. (Eagle-Lion). *Cast:* Dennis O'Keefe, Claire Trevor, Marsha Hunt, John Ireland, Raymond Burr. *VHS, LD ***

The Red House

(DELMER DAVES, 1947)

Sc.: Delmer Daves, from the novel by George Agnew Chamberlain. *Ph.:* Bert Glennon. *Mus.:* Miklos Rosza. *Prod.:* Sol Lesser for Thalia Productions. *Cast:* Edward G. Robinson, Lon McCallister, Judith Anderson, Allene Roberts, Julie London, Rory Calhoun, Ona Munson. *VHS ***

The Regeneration

(RAOUL WALSH, 1915)

Sc.: Raoul Walsh, Carl Harbaugh, from a play by Owen Kildare, Walter Hackett. *Ph.:* George Benoit. *Prod.:* William Fox. (Fox Film). *Cast:* Rockliffe Fellowes, Anna Q. Nilsson, William A. Sheer. *VHS ***

The Roaring Twenties

(RAOUL WALSH, 1939)

Sc.: Jerry Wald, Richard Macaulay, Robert Rossen, from a story by Mark Hellinger. *Ph.:* Ernest Haller. *Mus.:* Heinz Roemheld, Ray Heindorf. *Montages:* Don Siegel. *Prod.:* Mark Hellinger, Hal B. Wallis. (Warner Bros.). *Cast:* James Cagney, Priscilla Lane, Humphrey Bogart, Gladys George, Frank McHugh, Paul Kelly, Elizabeth Risdon. *VHS, LD*

The Robe

(HENRY KOSTER, 1953)

Sc.: Philip Dunne, from the novel by Lloyd C. Douglas, adapted by Gina Kaus. *Ph.:* Leon Shamroy (Technicolor, CinemaScope). *Mus.:* Alfred Newman. *Prod.:* Frank Ross. (20th Century-Fox). *Cast:* Richard Burton, Jean Simmons, Victor Mature, Michael Rennie, Jay Robinson, Dean Jagger, Torin Thatcher, Richard Boone, Betta St. John, Jeff Morrow, Ernest Thesiger, Dawn Addams. *VHS, LD*

Anthony Mann

Samson and Delilah

(CECIL B. DE MILLE, 1949)

Sc.: Jesse Lasky, Jr., Fredric M. Frank, from a story by Harold Lamb and Vladimir Jabotinsky. *Ph.:* George Barnes (Technicolor), Dewey Wrigley. *Mus.:* Victor Young. *Prod.:* Cecil B. De Mille. (Paramount). *Cast:* Hedy Lamarr, Victor Mature, George Sanders, Angela Lansbury, Henry Wilcoxon, Olive Deering, Fay Holden, Julia Faye, Russ Tamblyn, William Farnum. *VHS, LD*

Scarface

(HOWARD HAWKS, 1932)

Sc.: Ben Hecht, Seton I. Miller, John Lee Mahin, W. R. Burnett, Fred Palsey, from the novel by Armitage Trail. *Ph.:* Lee Garmes, L. William O'Connell. *Mus.:* Adolph Tandler, Gus Arnheim. *Prod.:* Howard Hughes, Howard Hawks for Atlantic Pictures. (United Artists). *Cast:* Paul Muni, Ann Dvorak, Karen Morley, Osgood Perkins, Boris Karloff, George Raft, Vince Barnett, C. Henry Gordon, Tully Marshall. *VHS, LD*

The Scarlet Empress

(JOSEF VON STERNBERG, 1934)

Sc.: Josef von Sternberg, from the diary of Catherine the Great, adapted by Manuel Komroff. *Ph.:* Bert Glennon. *Mus.:* W. Franke Harling, John M. Leipold, (and Joseph von Sternberg). *Prod.:* Adolph Zukor. (Paramount). *Cast:* Marlene Dietrich, John Lodge, Sam Jaffe, Louise Dresser, Gavin Gordon, C. Aubrey Smith, Maria Sieber, Ruthelma Stevens. *VHS* *

Scarlet Street

(FRITZ LANG, 1945)

Sc.: Dudley Nichols, from the novel and play *La Chienne* by Georges de la Fouchardiere in collaboration with Mouezy-Eon. *Ph.:* Milton Krasner. *Mus.:* Hans J. Salter. *Prod.:* Fritz Lang, Walter Wanger for Diana Productions. (Universal). *Cast:* Edward G. Robinson, Joan Bennett, Dan Duryea, Jess Barker, Margaret Lindsay, Rosalind Ivan. *VHS*

The Searchers

(JOHN FORD, 1956)

Sc.: Frank S. Nugent, from the novel by Alan LeMay. *Ph.:* Winton C. Hoch (Technicolor, VistaVision). *Mus.:* Max Steiner. *Prod.:* Merian C. Cooper. (Warner Bros.). *Cast:* John Wayne, Jeffrey Hunter, Vera Miles, Ward Bond, Natalie Wood, John Qualen, Olive Carey, Henry Brandon, Ken Curtis, Harry Carey, Jr., Hank Worden, Patrick Wayne. *VHS, LD*

Seventh Heaven

(FRANK BORZAGE, 1927)

Sc.: Benjamin Glazer, from the play by Austin Strong. *Titl.:* Katharine Hilliker, H.H. Caldwell. Ph.: Ernest Palmer. *Mus.:* William Perry. *Prod.:* Frank Borzage, Sol M. Wurtzel. (Fox Film). *Cast:* Janet Gaynor, Charles Farrell, Ben Bard, David Butler, Albert Gran, Gladys Brockwell, Emile Chautard, George Stone. *

She Wore a Yellow Ribbon

(JOHN FORD, 1949)

Sc.: Frank S. Nugent, Laurence Stallings, from the story "War Party" by James Warner Bellah. *Ph.:* Winton C. Hoch (Technicolor), Charles P. Boyle (2nd unit). *Mus.:* Richard Hageman. *2nd unit dir.:* Cliff Smith. *Prod.:* John Ford, Merian C. Cooper for Argosy Pictures. (RKO). *Cast:* John Wayne, Joanne Dru, John Agar, Ben Johnson, Harry Carey, Jr., Victor McLaglen. *VHS, LD*

Shock Corridor

(SAMUEL FULLER, 1963)

Sc.: Samuel Fuller, from his script "Straitjacket." *Ph.:* Stanley Cortez. *Mus.:* Paul Dunlap. *Prod.:* Samuel Fuller for Leon Fromkess—Sam Firks Productions. (Allied Artists). *Cast:* Peter Breck, Constance Towers, Gene Evans, James Best, Hari Rhodes, Larry Tucker. *VHS, LD*

Silver Lode

(ALLAN DWAN,1954)

Sc.: Karen De Wolfe. *Ph.:* John Alton (Technicolor). *Mus.:* Louis Forbes. *Prod.:* Benedict Bogeaus (RKO). *Cast:* John Payne, Dan Duryea, Lizabeth Scott, Dolores Moran, Emile Meyer, Harry Carey, Jr., Morris Ankrum, Robert Warwick, Stuart Whitman. *VHS* *

Some Came Running

(VINCENTE MINNELLI, 1958)

Sc.: John Patrick, Arthur Sheekman, from the novel by James Jones. *Ph.:* William H. Daniels (Metrocolor, CinemaScope). *Mus.:* Elmer Bernstein. *Prod.:* Sol C. Siegel. (MGM). *Cast:* Frank Sinatra, Dean Martin, Shirley MacLaine, Martha Hyer, Arthur Kennedy, Nancy Gates, Steven Peck. *VHS, LD*

Stagecoach

(JOHN FORD, 1939)

Sc.: Dudley Nichols, from the story "Stage to Lordsburg" by Ernest Haycox. *Ph.:* Bert Glennon. *Mus.:* Richard Hageman, W. Franke Harling, John Leipold, Leo Shuken, Louis Gruenberg. *2nd unit dir.:* Yakima Canutt. *Prod.:* John Ford, Walter Wanger. (United Artists). *Cast:* John Wayne, Claire Trevor, Thomas Mitchell, Andy Devine, John Carradine, Donald Meek, Louise Platt, George Bancroft, Berton Churchill, Tim Holt. *VHS, LD*

A Star is Born

(GEORGE CUKOR, 1954)

Sc.: Moss Hart, based on screenplay of 1937 nonmusical film by Dorothy Parker, Alan Campbell, Robert Carson, from story by William Wellman and Carson suggested by 1932 film *What Price Hollywood?* by Gene Fowler and Roland Brown from story by Adela Rogers St. Johns. *Ph.:* Sam Leavitt (Technicolor, CinemaScope). *Col. cons.:* George Hoyningen-Huene. *Prod. des.:* Gene Allen. *Mus.:* Harold Arlen. *Lyr.:* Ira Gershwin. *Chor.:* Richard Barstow. *Prod.:* Sidney Luft. (Warner Bros.). *Cast:* Judy Garland, James Mason, Jack Carson, Charles Bickford, Tommy Noonan. *VHS, LD*

A Streetcar Named Desire

(ELIA KAZAN, 1951)

Sc.: Tennessee Williams, adapted by Oscar Saul from Williams's play. *Ph.:* Harry Stradling. *Mus.:* Alex North. *Prod.:* Charles K. Feldman. (Warner Bros.). *Cast:* Vivien Leigh, Marlon Brando, Kim Hunter, Karl Malden, Rudy Bond, Nick Dennis. *VHS, LD* *

Sullivan's Travels

(PRESTON STURGES, 1941)

Sc.: Preston Sturges. *Ph.:* John B. Seitz. *Mus.:* Leo Shuken, Charles Bradshaw. *Prod.:* Paul Jones. (Paramount). *Cast:* Joel McCrea, Veronica Lake, Robert Warwick, William Demarest, Franklin Pangborn, Porter Hall, Byron Foulger, Margaret Hayes, Eric Blore. *VHS, LD* *

Sunrise

(F. W. MURNAU, 1927)

Sc.: Carl Mayer, from *The Journey to Tilsit* by Hermann Sudermann. *Titl.:* Katharine Hilliker, H. H. Caldwell. *Ph.:* Charles Rosher, Karl Struss. *Mus.:* Hugo Riesenfeld. *Prod. des.:* Rochus Gliese, Edgar G. Ulmer. *Prod.:* Fox Film. *Cast:* George O'Brien, Janet Gaynor, Margaret Livingstone, Bodil Rosing, J. Farrell Macdonald. *VHS*

Sweet Smell of Success

(ALEXANDER MACKENDRICK, 1957)

Sc.: Clifford Odets, adapted by Ernest Lehman from his short story "Tell Me About It Tomorrow." *Ph.:* James Wong Howe. *Mus.:* Elmer Bernstein. *Prod.:* James Hill for Norma-Curtleigh Productions. (United Artists). *Cast:* Burt Lancaster, Tony Curtis, Susan Harrison, Martin Milner, Sam Levene, Barbara Nichols, Jeff Donnell, Edith Atwater, Emile Meyer, Jay Adler. *VHS, LD*

The Tall T

(BUDD BOETTICHER, 1957)

Sc.: Burt Kennedy, from the story "The Captives" by Elmore Leonard. *Ph.:* Charles Lawton, Jr. (color by DeLuxe). *Mus.:* Heinz Roemheld. *Prod.:* Harry Joe Brown. (Columbia). *Cast:* Randolph Scott, Maureen O'Sullivan, Richard Boone, Arthur Hunnicutt, Skip Homeier, Henry Silva. *VHS* *

Elia Kazan

The Ten Commandments
(CECIL B. DE MILLE, 1923)

Sc.: Jeannie Macpherson. *Ph.:* J. Peverell Marley, Ray Rennahan (sequences in two-strip Technicolor). *Mus.:* Hugo Riesenfeld. *Prod.:* Paramount. *Cast:* Theodore Roberts, James Neill, Estelle Taylor, Charles De Rochefort, Richard Dix, Rod La Rocque, Edythe Chapman, Leatrice Joy. *VHS*

The Ten Commandments
(CECIL B. DE MILLE, 1956)

Sc: Aeneas MacKenzie, Jesse Lasky, Jr., Jack Gariss, Fredric M. Frank. *Ph.:* Loyal Griggs (Technicolor, Vistavision). *Mus.:* Elmer Bernstein. *Prod.:* Cecil B. De Mille. (Paramount). *Cast:* Charlton Heston, Yul Brynner, Anne Baxter, Edward G. Robinson, Yvonne De Carlo, Debra Paget, John Derek, Sir Cedric Hardwicke, Nina Foch, Martha Scott, Judith Anderson, Vincent Price, John Carradine, Olive Deering, Douglas Dumbrille, Henry Wilcoxon, H. B. Warner, Julia Faye. *VHS, LD*

T-Men
(ANTHONY MANN, 1948)

Sc.: John C. Higgins (and uncredited Anthony Mann), from a story by Virginia Kellogg. *Ph.:* John Alton. *Mus.:* Paul Sawtell. *Prod.:* Edward Small for Reliance Pictures. (Eagle-Lion). *Cast:* Dennis O'Keefe, Alfred Ryder, Mary Meade, Wallace Ford, June Lockhart, Charles McGraw, Jane Randolph. *VHS* *

2001: A Space Odyssey
(STANLEY KUBRICK, 1968)

Sc.: Stanley Kubrick, Arthur C. Clarke, from the short story "The Sentinel" by Clarke. *Ph.:* Geoffrey Unsworth (Technicolor-Metrocolor, Super Panavision 70 and Todd-AO); additional photography by: John Alcott. *Spec. photo. eff.:* Douglas Trumbull. *Prod. des.:* Tony Masters, Harry Lange, Ernest Archer. *Prod.:* Stanley Kubrick for Hawk Films. (MGM). Cast: Keir Dullea, Gary Lockwood, William Sylvester, Daniel Richter, Douglas Rain. *VHS, LD*

Two Weeks in Another Town
(VINCENTE MINNELLI, 1962)

Sc.: Charles Schnee, from the novel by Irwin Shaw. *Ph.:* Milton Krasner (Metrocolor, CinemaScope). *Mus.:* David Raksin. *Prod.:* John Houseman. (MGM). *Cast:* Kirk Douglas, Edward G. Robinson, Cyd Charisse, George Hamilton, Dahlia Lavi, Claire Trevor, Rosanna Schiaffino, Mino Doro. *LD* *

Unforgiven
(CLINT EASTWOOD, 1992)

Sc.: David Webb Peoples. *Ph.:* Jack N. Green (Technicolor, Panavision wide screen). *Prod. des.:* Henry Bumstead. *Mus.:* Lennie Niehaus. *Prod.:* Clint Eastwood for Malpaso. (Warner Bros.). *Cast:* Clint Eastwood, Gene Hackman, Morgan Freeman, Richard Harris, Jaime Woolvett, Saul Rubinek, Frances Fisher. *VHS, LD*

The Wedding March
(ERICH VON STROHEIM, 1927)

Sc.: Erich von Stroheim, Harry Carr. *Ph.:* Ben Reynolds, Hal Mohr. *Prod.:* P. A. Powers for the Famous Players-Lasky. (Paramount). *Cast:* Erich von Stroheim, Fay Wray, George Fawcett, Maude George, Cesare Gravina, Dale Fuller, Matthew Betz, Zasu Pitts. *VHS* *

Wild Boys of the Road
(WILLIAM WELLMAN, 1933)

Sc.: Earl Baldwin, from the story "Desperate Youth" by Danny Ahearn. *Ph.:* Arthur Todd. *Prod.:* Darryl F. Zanuck. (First National-Warner Bros.). *Cast:* Frankie Darro, Dorothy Coonan, Edwin Philips, Rochelle Hudson, Ann Hovey, Arthur Hohl, Ward Bond. *

CREDITS

A PERSONAL JOURNEY WITH MARTIN SCORSESE THROUGH AMERICAN MOVIES

A BFI Production for Channel 4, in association with Miramax Films

Written and Directed by Martin Scorsese and Michael Henry Wilson

Produced by Florence Dauman; Executive Producers: Colin McCabe, Bob Last

Supervising Editor: Thelma Schoonmaker; Editors: David Lindblom, Kenneth I. Levis

Associate Producer: Raffaele Donato; Line Producer: Dale Ann Stieber

Music: Elmer Bernstein

Titles: Saul Bass

Produced in Association with Cappa Productions.

Interviews: Frank Capra:, *Dialogue on Film*, AFI Seminar, 1979. King Vidor: *Dialogue on Film*, AFI Seminar, 1980. Howard Hawks: Hans Blumenberg's *A Hell of a Good Life*, Bayerischer Rundfunk, 1977. Fritz Lang: BBC Interview, 1967. Douglas Sirk: Interveiw by Mark Shiva, BBC, c1970. Nicholas Ray: Jim Gullman and Myron Meisel's *I'm a Stranger Here Myself*, 1974. Samuel Fuller: *Hollywood Mavericks*, AFI, 1989. Orson Welles: Interview by David Frost, Group W, 1970. Elia Kazan: Michel Ciment and Annie Tresgot's *Elia Kazan: Outsider*, Argos Films 1981. John Cassavetes: Michael Ventura's *I'm Almost Not Crazy*, Cannon, 1984. Francis Ford Coppola, Brian DePalma, André de Toth, Clint Eastwood, George Lucas, Gregory Peck, Arthur Penn and Billy Wilder interviewed for the BFI.

Photographs for the book courtesy of: Photofest; Archive Photos, Cahiers du Cinema, the British Film Institute, and the Museum of Modern Art Film Stills Library. Permission granted as follows: Disney/ABC International Television: *Duel in the Sun*. • Paramount Pictures: *The Furies*, copyright © 1950 by Paramount Pictures; *I Walk Alone*, copyright © 1948 by Paramount Pictures; *The Ten Commandments*, copyright © 1923 by Paramount Pictures; *The Ten Commandements*, copyright © 1956 by Paramount Pictures; *The Wedding March*, copyright © 1928 by Paramount Pictures. All Rights Reserved. • The Cadin Film Trust/IPMA: *Stagecoach* • Warner Bros.: *Barry Lyndon*, copyright © 1975 Warner Brothers, Inc.; *Bonnie and Clyde*, copyright © 1967, Warner Bros.-Seven Arts and Tatira-Hiller Productions; *Crime Wave*, copyright © 1954 Warner Bros. Pictures, Inc.; *East of Eden* © 1955 Warner Bros. Pictures, Inc.; *Gun Crazy* (aka *Deadly is the Female*); copyright © 1949 Pioneer Pictures Corporation; *Land of the Pharaohs*, copyright © 1955 The Continental Company Limited; *The Left-Handed Gun*, copyright © 1958 Warner Bros. Pictures, Inc.; *The Searchers* © 1956 Warner Bros. Pictures, Inc. *A Star is Born*, copyright © 1954 Warner Bros. Pictures, Inc.; *A Streetcar Named Desire*; copyright © 1951 Charles Feldman Group Productions; *Unforgiven*, copyright © 1992 Warner Bros., a division of Time Warner Entertainment Company, L. P. • Universal Studios Publishing Rights: All That Heaven Allows, copyright © 1997 by Universal City Studios, Inc.; Double Indemnity, copyright © 1997 by Universal City Studios; Scarface, copyright © 1997 by Universal City Studios, Inc.; *The Scarlet Empress:*, copyright © 1997 by Universal City Studios, Inc.; *Sullivan's Travels*, copyright ©1997 by Universal City Studios, Inc.; *Vertigo*, copyright © 1997 by Universal City Studios, Inc. All Rights Reserved. • Faces Distribution Group: *Faces*, , copyright © Faces International Films, Inc. • MGM Consumer Products: *Kiss Me Deadly*, copyright © 1955 Parklane Pictures, Inc.; *One, Two, Three*, copyright © 1961 The Mirisch Company, Inc.; *Sweet Smell of Success*, copyright © 1957 Norma-Curtleight Productions, Inc., All Rights Reserved. • Broadway Video, L.P.: *T-Men* • Columbia Pictures: *On the Waterfront*; *The Tall T* • Otto Preminger Films, Ltd.: *The Man with the Golden Arm* • Ben Barry & Associates, Inc.: *The Naked Kiss, Shock Corridor* • Turner Entertainment Co.: *Anna Christie*, copyright © 1930 Turner Entertainment Co.; *The Bad and the*

Note: Film stills do not replicate the correct proportions of the screen. The Cinemascope screen is wider and shorter than the stills on pages 88, 90-93.

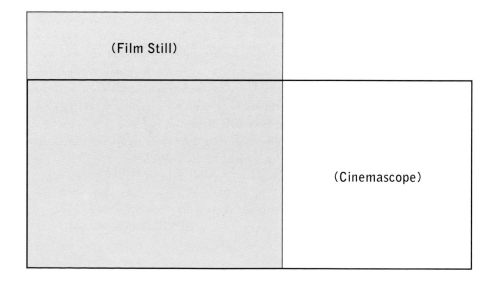